MW01199600

Weir

NORTH CAROLINA TRIVIA

John V. Wood & Lisa Wojna

BLUE
BIKE
BOOKS

The Publisher: Blue Bike Books
Website: www.bluebikebooks.com

Library and Archives Canada Cataloguing in Publication

Wood, John V., 1972–
North Carolina trivia / John V. Wood and Lisa Wojna.

ISBN 978-1-926700-30-4

1. North Carolina—Miscellanea. I. Wojna, Lisa, 1962–
   II. Title.

F254.6.W663 2010   975.6   C2010-900747-6

Project Director: Nicholle Carrière
Project Editor: Nicholle Carrière
Cover Image: Photos.com
Illustrations: Craig Howrie, Roger Garcia, Peter Tyler, Patrick Hénaff

We acknowledge the support of the Alberta Foundation for the Arts for our publishing program.
We acknowledge the financial support of the Government of Canada through the Book Publishing Industry Development Program (BPIDP) for our publishing activities.

Canadian   Patrimoine
Heritage   canadien

PC: 5

DEDICATION

This book is dedicated to my lovely wife, Cinnamon. You have always inspired me to be the best writer I can be and have always made me want to be a better husband. I love you more than my words can ever say.

–John V. Wood

CONTENTS

INTRODUCTION 8

NORTH CAROLINA'S WOW FACTOR
What Sets North Carolina Apart? 10

SYMBOLS OF THE STATE
Just the Facts 15
Inanimate State Symbols 19
Living (or Previously Living) State Symbols 29

GEOGRAPHY
The Lay of the Land 33
County Curiosities 38

CLIMATE AND WEATHER
Averages and Extremes 59

WILD LIFE
Animals 65
Feathered Friends 71
Here Fishy, Fishy 74
Plant Life 77

POPULATION INFORMATION
By the Numbers 80

TOURISM
Roadside Attractions 89
Must-See NC 96
Ghost Stories and Folk Legends 103

HISTORICAL HAPPENINGS
The Lost Colony 108
Founding Fathers and Flyers 113
Notable Events 116

COMMUNITIES
The Name Game 118
Claim Fame 120

ECONOMY
Crunching the Numbers 124
Planes, Trains and Automobiles! 126
Got To Be NC Agriculture 130

Other Economic Mother Lodes 134

LIFESTYLE
General Health and Wellness 138
Drugs, Booze and All Things Naughty 143
Best in Barbecue 149

EDUCATION
Oldest Schools 151
North Carolina's Public Schools 153
Higher Learning 156
Notable People and Events 163

POLITICS
Division of Power 167
Notable Figures 170
Underground Movements 174

THE ARTS
Painters and Sculptors 177
Music and Entertainment 181
TV, Radio and Print 186
Literature 189
Architecture and Design 193
Birthplace: North Carolina 196

SCIENCE AND TECHNOLOGY
Blinded Me with Science 201
Inventions, Discoveries and Breakthroughs 205

LAW AND CRIME
Long Arm of the Law 210
Local Laws of Interest 213
Most Dangerous Places 215
(In)Famous Criminals 217

SPORTS
Notable Sports Figures and Record Breakers 223
Notable Moments in Sports 231
Popular Sports in the State 235

OTHER MISCELLANEOUS FIRSTS AND FACTS
First and Foremost 245

LAST BUT NOT LEAST
Top 10 Reasons to Live in North Carolina 250

ACKNOWLEDGMENTS

It would be virtually impossible for me to thank everyone who helped in the writing of this book. However, ask my wife… hearing the word "impossible" has never stopped me before.

To Nicholle at Blue Bike Books: Working with you was so much fun, and I enjoyed your insight into the process!

To my co-author, Lisa Wojna: You are truly a special person. Your contributions to this book were immeasurable, and it was a pleasure to work with you!

To my wonderful family (Cinnamon, Dillon, Skye, Paige, Hermione, et al): Without you, my food has no flavor. Without you, my world has no color. Without you, this book would never have been finished. I cannot express my complete gratitude for everything you've done for me during the writing of this book. I owe everything to you, and I hope you understand how much I love you.

To my niece, Stephanie: your enthusiasm is contagious. Thanks for the inspiration over three-cheese chicken penne.

To the Triangle Area Freelancers writers' group: Taffies, you guys heard about this book from the very beginning. Thanks for being there every step of the way. Thanks also to Don Vaughan, my mentor and the founder of TAF. You never let the writing stop. Thank you for that.

To everyone else who has ever lived, worked, dared to dream or changed anything about North Carolina over the years: Without your innovation, your chutzpah, your inspiration, this book would not be worth reading.

–John V. Wood

Many thanks to our clever editor, who pieced together the work of two authors and did so seamlessly; to my co-author, John; and to my family—my husband Garry, sons Peter, Matthew and Nathan, daughters Melissa and Jada, and grandson Seth. Without you, all this and anything else I do in my life would be meaningless.

–Lisa Wojna

INTRODUCTION

When I started writing this book, I felt it would be fairly easy for two reasons—one, I was born and raised in North Carolina; and two, I'm a history buff with a flair for trivial knowledge. Seemed like a perfect fit. I had only been back in North Carolina since 2003 (I spent seven years traveling the United States—Washington, Nevada, Georgia—as a television journalist), so what better way to relearn the state that I'm proud to call my home? Funny thing is, as I compiled my research, I was learning about things I had never heard of, never seen or never even imagined. Texas Pete Hot Sauce started in North Carolina—imagine that! A state that I had prided myself on knowing the ins-and-outs of, the intricate details that made her what she is, and I had no idea there was so much more to the Tar Heel State.

Much of this state's majestic attraction is rooted in her history, being one of the 13 original colonies (I had to sing a song about that in the third grade for May Day—oh, the memories). One can also argue that North Carolina is best known in the sports world (Tobacco Road, NASCAR, golf) and for the athletic specimens the state has produced over the years (Michael Jordan, Richard Petty, Arnold Palmer).

One of the best things about this book is that it (hopefully) keeps your interest. So many history or fact-based books are boring in that they just dump information in your lap. I'd like to think that the tone of this book is a little informal, as if we were sitting on a front porch in Johnston County, drinking sweet tea and telling stories about the first things that pop into our minds. That's what I was aiming for, anyway. And *Dragnet*, it's not. It's not just about facts and figures. There are some personal elements thrown in, experiences I've had with the topics included. It's not just about the thing itself; the feelings attached are important, too.

Over the course of this venture, I have fallen in love with this state all over again. I've seen the good things, and I've suffered through the less than stellar. A perfect state would be boring. A state with bumps and bruises has personality and shows how strong people deal with the issues, get up and move on. I have found some of the quirkiest things imaginable and I'm proud to be able to share them with you now. Can you imagine that, in the same state, you can find the nation's oldest grapevine (the Mothervine), the world's oldest mountain range (the Appalachians) and the best barbecue known to man (sorry, Memphis and Kansas City)?

Hopefully, as you read this book, you'll begin to understand the reasons why North Carolina is one of the best states in the Union. From Manteo to Murphy, the state has it all. It would have been impossible to include every interesting tidbit or morsel in this book, unless you'd rather the book be about 1000 pages long. I just hope the information contained inside these pages informs, entertains and persuades you to come and visit the Old North State.

I'm glad I call North Carolina home.

–John V. Wood

WHAT SETS NORTH CAROLINA APART?

All-Access

The great thing about North Carolina is its complete access to everything! You have beaches, mountains, lakes, rivers, gardens, parks—all within a day's drive! One of North Carolina's slogans is that you can find anything between Manteo and Murphy (the state's eastern and westernmost cities, respectfully). You could leave Mt. Mitchell in Anson County after breakfast, drive through Pisgah National Forest, stop at Jordan Lake for lunch and then get to Calabash for some awesome seafood on the coast by dinnertime! That whole trip would take about eight hours, not including bathroom breaks or necessary photo opportunities.

Got to be NC Agriculture

North Carolina has long been an agricultural state. The state leads the nation in the production of flue-cured tobacco, sweet potatoes and Christmas trees. It is second in the production of hogs, pigs, trout and turkeys. North Carolina also exported more than $3.1 billion worth of agricultural products in 2008.

"Real" Barbecue

North Carolina has long been embattled with Memphis and Kansas City for BBQ bragging rights. The North Carolina BBQ Society calls the state the "Cradle of 'Cue," and Tar Heel residents can argue about the superiority of their 'cue all day long. People here also believe that you do not "barbecue" something—you "grill" it. "Barbecue" can only be used as a noun or an adjective—not a verb.

Hook, Line and Sinker

North Carolina has some of the best saltwater and freshwater fishing in the country, attracting people from all over the United States. The world's largest red drum (94 pounds, 2 ounces) was caught by David Deuel in 1984 near Cape Hatteras. Other world-record saltwater fish caught here include the bluefish (31 pounds, 12 ounces), hogfish (21 pounds, 6 ounces), Spanish mackerel (13 pounds even) and sand tilefish (4 pounds, 5 ounces).

A Light in the Storm

North Carolina's coast is home to many lighthouses, most of which are still in operation. Cape Hatteras Lighthouse, one of the most recognized in history, is the only lighthouse ever to be moved because of erosion concerns. The current Bodie (pronounced *body*) Island Lighthouse is actually the third version; the previous two washed away when Oregon Inlet shifted southward.

Capital Cities

North Carolina has several self-proclaimed "capitals of the world":

Antiques: Cameron

Barbecue: Lexington

Billfish: Outer Banks

Chair: Thomasville

Clogging: Maggie Valley

Firefly: Boone

Gem: Franklin

Golf: Pinehurst

Hollerin': Spivey's Corner

Home Furnishings: High Point

NASCAR: Mooresville

Opossum: Brasstown

Pottery: Seagrove

Sailing: Oriental

Salamander: Great Smoky Mountains

Seafood: Calabash

Whistling: Louisburg

Tee It Up!

North Carolina has long been considered one of the premier golfing destinations in the country. The site of more championships than any other golf course in the country since 1898, Pinehurst welcomes back the U.S. Open and U.S. Women's Open Championships in 2014. North Carolina has more than 550 courses (including both public-access and private courses) to choose from, so grab your 1 Wood and let's hit the links!

Tobacco Road

Okay, North Carolina may have a lot to offer, but collegiate athletics rank among the most well known. My sister-in-law moved to Seattle, and when her co-workers found out where she was from, one said, "Oh, you must be a basketball fan." Between Carolina, NC State, Duke and Wake Forest, most of the state shuts down for March Madness. It's tough when three of the best college basketball programs in the country are all less than 30 miles apart.

Pour Yourself a Glass

The grape vine was introduced to the New World not long after the English landed at Roanoke. Ever since, grapes have flourished in NC's soil, and wineries have sprouted up all across the state. By the dawn of the 20th century, North Carolina had become the leading wine-producing state in the country. If you've never had a homegrown scuppernong, then you haven't truly lived.

DID YOU  KNOW?

Congress changed North Carolina's wine status with a little thing called Prohibition. During Prohibition, moonshine (homemade alcohol) runners raced across the North Carolina countryside, trying to sell their wares and stay a few miles ahead of the Highway Patrol. That speedy mentality led to the invention of the pastime now known as NASCAR.

Built To Be More
In 1889, George Washington Vanderbilt II set out to build a summer escape near Asheville, where his mother, Maria, lived. When it was completed, in 1895, the Biltmore House was a sprawling, 175,000-square-foot, 250-room private home on an estate that includes some 8000 acres of land—some sources have dubbed it the "largest private home in the world." By the 1930s, during the height of the Great Depression, Cornelia Stuyvesant Vanderbilt and her husband, John Cecil, decided it would be prudent to open the home to the public and operate it as a kind of living museum. In 1964, it was named a National Historic Landmark, and in 2007, it was listed in eighth position in the American Institute of Architects' top 150 favorites of American architecture. The Biltmore is still family owned.

JUST THE FACTS

What's in a Name?

Originally there was only one Carolina, and the name chosen for the new colony honored three men named Charles: Charles IX of France and England's Charles I and Charles II. The English name Charles is derived from the Latin name Carolinus. The colony of Carolina was divided into North and South Carolina in 1729.

Also Known As

North Carolina has several nicknames: the Rip Van Winkle State, the Turpentine State, the Old North State, the Land of the Sky and the Tar Heel State. Of course, each moniker brings with it an interesting story:

☛ There are a couple of variations on the story of how North Carolina came by the name the Tar Heel State. One has to do with the abundance of tar and its effects on the economy in the state's early years. Another variation plays with the idea that it was neglect that caused North Carolina soldiers to falter in their battle against Mississippians—they hadn't "tarred their heels," and therefore couldn't "stick" their ground. Yet another theory as to the origin of this nickname, and a variation on the previous tale, has the North Carolina soldiers bantering with their opposition about the availability of tar in the state. According to this version, by Walter Clark, the soldiers suggested that their opponents put the tar on their heels so they could "stick better in the next fight."

☛ The Land of the Sky moniker came from the book of the same title written by Frances Fisher Tieran in 1876. The name is also found in the state's official toast.

☛ The appellation the Old North State makes a frequent appearance in the state toast. A boundary line dividing Carolina into northern and southern regions existed in 1710, and this nickname naturally referred to the northern part of the state.

☛ Turpentine was a natural by-product created from the harvested oleoresin of the slash and longleaf pine trees, and in the early years of this state, North Carolina had a plethora of these pines. Turpentine was an important component in the naval stores industry and an important component in a healthy economy for the state. Hence the nickname the Turpentine State.

☛ Exactly how North Carolina acquired the nickname the Rip Van Winkle State is one of the state's most enduring mysteries.

At least one source suggests that the name was adopted some time in the 1800s, after the short story "Rip Van Winkle," written by Washington Irving, was published in 1819.

Making It Official

North Carolina was the 12th state to be admitted to the Union. It was officially declared a state on November 21, 1789.

Capital City
The city of Raleigh was established in 1792, but the site was selected for the establishment of the state's capital years earlier, in 1788. One of the drawing cards for this decision by the founding fathers of North Carolina was its central location.

Rally Cry
According to one source, North Carolina has two commonly used slogans: "A Better Place to Be" and "First in Flight," a saying that's embedded in the state's license plates. Another more humorous slogan bandied about is "Tobacco is a Vegetable."

State Motto

North Carolina's state motto is probably one of the most unique in the country. If nothing else, "To be, rather than to seem," is a motto that will get folks philosophizing.

Seal of Approval
The Great Seal of North Carolina is the result of final design changes adopted in 1983. And though much of the current design reflects the original, there have been several changes throughout the years. The first standardization of North Carolina's seal was initiated in 1971. Reviewing all previous versions, it was decided that the official seal would measure two and one-quarter inches in diameter. The figures of the seal are Liberty, holding her pole, a cap perched on its top in her left hand and a scroll with the word "Constitution" in her

right hand, and Plenty, sitting alongside the horn of plenty with three stalks of grain in her right hand and her left hand leaning on the narrow end of the horn. These two women face each other on either side of the seal, and in the background are mountains on the left and, on the right, a ship with three masts. Around the outer circumference of the seal are the words "The Great Seal of North Carolina" and the Latin words *Esse Quam Videri*. The Latin phrase refers to the state's motto, "To be, rather than to seem."

Two dates appear on the seal: May 20, 1775, is top and center, and refers to what's called the Mecklenburg Declaration of Independence. The second date, April 12, 1776, centered on the bottom of the seal, was added in 1983. It represents the date of the adoption of the Halifax Resolves, a declaration that has been called a stepping-stone on the way to the formation and signing of the United States Declaration of Independence.

If You're From Here
Folks in North Carolina are known as North Carolinians.

North Carolina Sayings

If the following sayings are any indication, folks in this state know how to laugh at themselves:

☛ You know you're from North Carolina if you've ever turned on the heat and the air-conditioning in the same day.

☛ North Carolina is the place you fly over on the way to Florida. (John Fleischman)

☛ You know you're from North Carolina if you ordered your hot dog or burger "all the way." ("All the way" means with mustard, chili and slaw.)

INANIMATE STATE SYMBOLS

Flying High

There was no official recognition of North Carolina's state flag until May 20, 1861. The official ordinance, introduced into the legislature by Colonel John D. Whitford, stated, "the flag of this State shall be a blue field with a white "V" thereon, and a star, encircling which shall be the words, *Sirgit astrum*, May 20, 1775."

Raleigh-based artist William Jarl Browne was asked for his professional thoughts on the design, and on June 22, Browne presented Whitford and the committee of seven assigned to the project with an altogether different design proposal. Browne's version divided the flag into three sections: a solid red bar running vertically across one-third of the left side of the flag, with the remaining two-thirds divided horizontally, with white on the bottom portion and blue on the top portion. The May 20, 1775 date was centered in the red portion of the flag, surrounding a white, five-pointed star. Beneath the star was the date May 20, 1861—the date that North Carolina seceded from the Union. This flag was the banner raised by North Carolina soldiers battling the Confederacy during the Civil War.

In 1864, after the Civil War, the state reworked the design of its flag. The red field on the left of the flag was changed to blue, and red replaced the top horizontal bar along the white bottom. The initial date of the Mecklenburg Declaration of Independence remained, but the bottom date was changed to April 12, 1776, the date of the Halifax Resolves. Both dates were placed within a gold ribbon that arched, above and beneath, the gilt letters *N* and *C,* and the five-pointed, white star between them.

North Carolina
NUGGET

On May 4, 2007, North Carolina passed Bill No. 258, acknowledging the following statement as the state's official salute to its flag: "I salute the flag of North Carolina and pledge to the Old North State love, loyalty and faith."

The Tar Heel Toast

North Carolina adopted an official state toast in 1957, using a poem written in 1904 by Leonora Martin and Mary Burke Kerr for the purpose. Officially titled "A Toast to North Carolina," legend has it that this patriotic rhyme was nicknamed "The Tar Heel Toast," but at least one source suggests that there's no direct reference to that moniker in official records. While it's more common to hear the first verse recited, it would be fun to see how many folks can recite all the words:

Here's to the land of the long leaf pine,
The summer land where the sun doth shine,
Where the weak grow strong and the strong grow great,
Here's to "Down Home," the Old North State!

Here's to the land of the cotton bloom white,
Where the scuppernong perfumes the breeze at night,
Where the soft southern moss and jessamine mate,
'Neath the murmuring pines of the Old North State!

Here's to the land where the galax grows,
Where the rhododendron's rosette glows,
Where soars Mount Mitchell's summit great,
In the "Land of the Sky," in the Old North State!

Here's to the land where maidens are fair,
Where friends are true and cold hearts rare,
The near land, the dear land, whatever fate,
The blest land, the best land, the Old North State!

Singing Loud, Singing Proud

North Carolina's state song is aptly named "The Old North State." William Joseph Gaston wrote the words to this beloved song some time before his death in 1844, but it wasn't adopted as the state's official song until February 27, 1927. At that time, it was also recognized as the state's official toast until "The Tar Heel Toast" received its designation in 1957. With five verses and a chorus repeated between, North Carolina's state song is quite lengthy. But the verses combine to tell a patriotic story that needs to be heard in its entirety.

The Old North State

Verse 1
Carolina! Carolina! Heaven's blessings attend her!
While we live we will cherish, protect and defend her;
Though the scorner may sneer at and witlings defame her,
Our hearts swell with gladness whenever we name her.

Chorus
Hurrah! Hurrah! The Old North State forever!
Hurrah! Hurrah! The good Old North State!

Verse 2
Though she enview not others their merited glory,
Say, whose name stands the foremost in Liberty's story!

Though too true to herself e'er to crouch to oppression,
Who can yield to just rule more loyal submission?

Verse 3
Plain and artless her sons, but whose doors open faster
At the knock of a stranger, or the tale of disaster?
How like to the rudeness of their dear native mountains,
With rich ore in their bosoms and life in their fountains.

Verse 4
And her daughters, the Queen of the Forest resembling—
So graceful, so constant, yet to gentlest breath trembling;
And true lightwood at heart, let the match be applied them,
How they kindle and flame! Oh! None know but who've tried
them.

Verse 5
Then let all who love us, love the land that we live in
As happy a region on this side of Heaven,
Where Plenty and Freedom, Love and Peace smile before us,
Raise aloud, raise together, the heart-thrilling chorus!"

The Perfect Food

With a plethora of nutrients such as calcium, phosphorus, potassium and vitamin A, is it any wonder that milk is considered the perfect food. It only makes sense that this favorite accompaniment to cookies was named North Carolina's official state beverage in 1987. In fact, milk is such a popular drink that it's been named as either an official state beverage or official state drink in a total of 19 states, if you include Rhode Island's choice of "coffee milk."

Saying It in Color
North Carolina is one of only 11 states that have adopted official colors for the state—and the legislature chose a very patriotic blue and red for this particular honor.

State Quarter

Each state boasts a state quarter, and North Carolina was the 12th state to design theirs. The commemorative quarter, adopted in 2001, celebrates the "first flight" conducted by Orville and Wilbur Wright on December 17, 1903.

State Boat

As a seaside state, it only makes sense that North Carolina would have adopted an official state boat to add to their list of significant symbols. In 1987, the shad boat was given this designation because of the importance it played as a workboat in the early days of the state. The long, narrow but deep vessel is both versatile and easy to maneuver. The shad boat was named after the American or Atlantic shad, a fish that is related to the herring family. Fishermen harvesting these fish used the shad boat.

Festivals Galore

Not only is there a wide assortment of festivals happening all over North Carolina at any given time of the year, but the state has also recognized several with special designations:

☛ The **Lexington Barbecue Festival** was named the state's Food Festival of the Piedmont Triad Region of the State of North Carolina in 2007. The first Lexington event was held on October 27, 1984, and it met with such huge success that it's been held on one of the last two Saturdays in October ever since. The original Barbecue Festival drew crowds of about 30,000 people, and it was estimated that about 3000 pounds of food was cooked. Since 2003, more than 150,000 people have visited Lexington's festival, which takes place along an eight-block stretch of Main Street.

☛ In 1975, the idea of establishing some kind of annual festival for Ayden was bandied about and publicized with a letter to the editor and a discussion between Willis E. Manning Jr., the president of the Chamber of Commerce at the time, and the then-editor of the *Ayden-NewsLeader*. An ad-hoc committee was formed to further iron out the idea, and from its efforts, six themes were isolated: a collard festival, a cucumber festival, a "Garden of Ayden Almost-Paradise," a harvest festival, a "Progressive Ayden Day" or a "September Fun Festival." The idea of celebrating collard greens won out, and the first Ayden Collard Festival was held on September 13, 1975. Today, more than 30 years later, the festival continues to be a community-building event that draws visitors from far and wide every September, from the Tuesday after Labor Day through to Saturday. Collard greens play a prominent role in the event, with a collard-cooking-and-eating contest, which is usually held on the Saturday. The **Ayden Collard Festival** was named the state's official collard festival in 2007.

☛ For two weeks at the end of every July, the community of Waynesville hosts a festival celebrating the diversity of cultural backgrounds represented in its community and throughout the country. The first **Folkmoot USA Festival** was held in 1984, in conjunction with North Carolina's 400th birthday, and it immediately became an annual event. Since that first festival, the heritage of more than 100 countries has been explored and celebrated. One of the festival's mandates is to acquire an entirely new slate of programs and performers each year, which has kept the event fresh and exciting for residents and visitors alike. Folkmoot USA was named North Carolina's official international festival in 2003.

☛ Elizabeth City is home to North Carolina's official Irish Potato Festival. The **Albemarle Potato Festival** received this designation in 2009.

☛ The watermelon—sweet, juicy and a darned good reason to celebrate. Every year, Murfreesboro hosts North Carolina's annual watermelon festival. In 1993, the state recognized the

Hertford County Watermelon Festival as its official Northeastern Watermelon Festival.

☛ Not to be outdone, Fair Bluff was recognized for its efforts to promote the watermelon—or summer festivals in general—also in 1993. That's when the state recognized the **Fair Bluff Watermelon Festival** as its official Southeastern Watermelon Festival. Gotta love those watermelons!

Proud Plaid

North Carolina's official tartan is none other than the Carolina Tartan. It's a happy-looking, colorful plaid with light blue, green, yellow and white overlaid on red, its most prominent color. It was recognized as the state's official tartan in 1991.

Dance Away!
North Carolina has two official state dances:

☛ In 2005, clogging—a traditional American folk dance with roots in a variety of ethnic traditions, including African American, Cherokee, French and British—was named North Carolina's official folk dance. Traditional cloggers wear wooden-bottomed, leather shoes and keep the beat with the slapping and stamping of their feet.

☛ Also in 2005, North Carolina named the shag as its official popular dance. The partnered dance can be performed to just about any kind of music and consists of a complicated series of steps. Experts at the dance are mesmerizing to watch and look like they're almost floating along the ground.

Glorious Green
The state legislature chose the emerald as the state's official precious stone in 1973. The emerald is one of more than 300 minerals found throughout the North Carolina country-side, and the state made history when James K. Hill found

what many would argue was the largest emerald to have ever been discovered in North America. The stone, measuring about 18.8 carats and named the Carolina Queen Emerald, was unearthed in Hiddenite in 1998.

Hard as Rock

The largest open-face granite quarry in the world operates in the heart of North Carolina. The North Carolina Granite Corporation is located in Mount Airy, and stone has been harvested from the site for more than 150 years.

North Carolina NUGGET Mount Airy was the setting for the popular television show *Mayberry*, starring none other than Mount Airy's own Andy Griffith. Every year, the town hosts a cast reunion during Mayberry Days.

Speaking the Language
North Carolina's official state language is English. While this is the primary language for the majority of the population, it didn't receive this distinction until 1987.

Atten-tion!

The Oak Ridge Military Academy in Oak Ridge was named the state's official military academy in 1991.

Pretty as a Picture

Keep your eyes peeled as you stroll along North Carolina's coastal shorelines and you might find one of these lovely specimens washed up on the beach. The Scotch bonnet, a hearty yet beautiful cream-and-orange shell that twirls around like a treble clef, was designated the state's official shell in 1965.

Curtain!

The Thalian Association in Wilmington traces its roots back to 1788, when it was established to bring the finer things of life to a new and growing city. For more than 221 years, the theatre has showcased the best of the performing arts. In 2007, the Thalian Association was named the state's official community theater.

LIVING (OR PREVIOUSLY LIVING) STATE SYMBOLS

Juicy Fruit

North Carolina is definitely fond of its fruit. The state has recognized three fruits for special distinction: the blueberry is the official blue berry of the state; the strawberry is its official red berry; and the scuppernong grape is North Carolina's official fruit.

Sing-Along

The cardinal was named North Carolina's official state bird in 1943. The red-beaked, red-feathered bird with a spiked crown is not only striking in appearance, but its "purdy, purdy, purdy, whoit, whoit, whoit" call will also alert any avid birder to its presence.

Come a Little Closer...

Just because it's pretty and pink doesn't mean it's not dangerous. Any insect that ventures too close to this lovely, leafy plant risks being a snack. The carnivorous Venus flytrap lives on the insects and creepy-crawlies that mosey on by, thinking the plant is just another delicate patch of greenery. The Venus flytrap not only catches its prey between its pretty pink pads, but it also digests it within 12 hours and is ready to catch the next unsuspecting bug. Interestingly enough, the Venus flytrap is only native to the Carolinas. North Carolina recognized this unique fact by naming the Venus flytrap as its official state carnivorous plant in 2005.

Wooden Wonder

The Fraser fir, also known as *Abies fraseri*, is a species of fir unique to the eastern U.S. and, in particular, North Carolina. The rather small evergreen, which is quite prominent in the western part of the state, was named North Carolina's official Christmas tree in 2005.

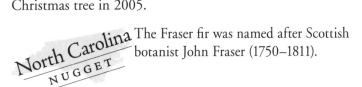 The Fraser fir was named after Scottish botanist John Fraser (1750–1811).

Proud Pooch
Folks in North Carolina are well aware that a dog is man's best friend. In fact, the state legislature was so convinced of the value of these four-legged companions that it named the Plott hound as the state's official dog in 1989. Athletic, muscular and with eyes that will make you just melt, the Plott hound is a perfect companion and a great coonhound.

Blossoming Beauty

Although North Carolinians have always loved the dogwood, according to the April 1917 issue of *National Geographic* magazine, it was the daisy that was North Carolina's state flower. Apparently, the favorite-flower tug-of-war was an ongoing battle, and in the 1936 issue of *Flower Grower Magazine*, the nomination of the oxeye daisy as the possible official state flower had been defeated, and some folks were tossing about the idea of naming the goldenrod to the honored position. In the late 1930s, the daisy and the goldenrod were up against the flame azalea, the dogwood, the Venus flytrap and the pinecone for the position of state flower. For a long time, it was a toss-up between the dogwood and the flame azalea, but the dogwood eventually won out, partly because it's so common throughout the state. On March 15, 1941, the dogwood was officially named the state flower.

One and Only
"One of a kind" is a pretty special distinction in and of itself, but the Southern Appalachian strain of brook trout is more than the state's only native freshwater trout. It was named the state's official freshwater trout on September 13, 2005, much to the delight of North Carolina's sport fishermen.

Freshwater Fish

The channel bass, another favorite among anglers, was elevated to the position of official state freshwater fish in 1971.

Busy as a Bee
The lively, yellow-and-black-striped bumblebee is as recognizable throughout North America as the mosquito. The honey-producer is a lot sweeter, though, and that certainly was one of the things that made it a great candidate for the state's official insect. In 1973, it was officially given that distinction.

Industrious Critter

The gray squirrel has reigned as the state's official mammal since 1969. It is common throughout the state but especially loves the swamps of eastern North Carolina and the upland hardwood forests of the Piedmont and the western counties.

Slow and Steady

Mother Nature endowed the eastern box turtle with a beautifully designed shell that can completely close off the reptile's vulnerable body from any predators. In the wild, these turtles can survive for eight decades, and although they are popular as pets, they don't fare as well in captivity, where their life expectancy is shortened by three to five decades. In 1979, North Carolina named the eastern box turtle the official state reptile.

Tall and Stately

The pine tree was rightly awarded the designation of official state tree in 1963. It is numbered among North Carolina's most common trees, but that's not the only reason for naming it to this honor. The pine was a staple in the state's economy, providing resin, turpentine and timber.

Sweet Spuds

What Thanksgiving banquet would be complete without the sweet potato? Use it for dessert or the main entrée—either way, it's amazing. In 1995, it was designated North Carolina's official state vegetable.

Long and Lean

The Carolina lily was designated the state's official wildflower in 2003. Each plant may have as many as six red-orange blooms on long stems that tower as much as four feet off the ground.

THE LAY OF THE LAND

How Big?

North Carolina measures 500 miles in length and about 150 miles in width, covering a total area of 53,864 square miles. That makes this southern location the 28th largest state in the country.

Solid Ground
Of North Carolina's total geography, 48,708 square miles are land areas.

Water, Water, Everywhere?
Only 9.5 percent of North Carolina's total area, or about 5103 square miles, is covered in water. The state also has about 301 miles of coastline.

Breaking It Down

The topography of the most westerly fifth of North Carolina is made up of rolling foothills and the Blue Ridge and Great Smoky mountains. The central two-fifths of the state is largely composed of the 200-mile-wide Piedmont plateau, a geographic feature that stretches along eight eastern states, from New Jersey to Alabama. And the eastern two-fifths of the state, bordering the Atlantic Ocean, is categorized as the Coastal Plain and Tidewater region.

Dead Center

Were you to drive to the exact geographic center of the state, you'd find yourself in Lee County, about 10 miles northwest of Sanford.

High Point

With a peak of 6684 feet, Mount Mitchell is the highest point in the state. Located in the Black Mountains, it was named in honor of Dr. Elisha Mitchell. The University of North Carolina science professor explored the area in 1835 in an effort to measure the area's mountains. It was commonly believed that Grandfather Mountain was the state's tallest peak, but Mitchell believed his namesake was higher. He made several calculations through a succession of mathematical formulas, and his last estimate placed Mount Mitchell a mere 12 feet shy of today's calculations.

 Dr. Elisha Mitchell died in 1857 while hiking in the Black Mountains. Mount Mitchell received its name in 1858.

Low Point
I'll put money on it that with a little thought, just about everyone could identify North Carolina's lowest geographic point. If you guessed that it's the state's Atlantic coastline, which would be sea level, you'd be correct.

Middle of the Road
Number crunchers have identified North Carolina's mean elevation at 700 feet above sea level.

The Rivers Roll Through It
☛ The Neuse, Cape Fear, Roanoke and Yadkin are North Carolina's major rivers.

☛ The Neuse River measures about 195 miles in length and snakes its way through seven of North Carolina's 100 counties. The size of the Neuse watershed is 6235 square miles and covers 73 municipalities.

☛ The Cape Fear River, which is 202 miles in length, is the only river in North Carolina that flows directly into the Atlantic Ocean. It is also the state's largest river basin (9149 square miles). This river flows through 29 of the state's 100 counties and is the longest river to run entirely inside the state's boundaries.

☛ More than 200 species of birds make their home along the Roanoke River. The watershed covers about 3600 square miles, and the river is about 410 miles long.

☛ The Yadkin River is 435 miles long and is a prime destination for canoeing enthusiasts. It is known as the "Tigris and Euphrates of the Carolinas" because human civilization has existed along the river for over 12,000 years. The Yadkin watershed covers over 7213 square miles.

DID YOU KNOW?

The New River, which begins in Ashe County and travels through Virginia and West Virginia, is considered by some geologists to be the second-oldest river in the world, somewhere between 10 million and 360 million years old.

Great Lakes

According to the state's fishing enthusiasts, there are 1938 lakes, ponds, reservoirs and other fishing bodies of water where you can drop a line. North Carolina's major lakes are Lake Mattamuskeet, Lake Phelps and Lake Waccamaw.

☛ The first recorded discovery of Lake Mattamuskeet took place on July 11, 1585, when members of Sir Walter Raleigh's Roanoke Island expedition passed through the area. It is North Carolina's largest natural lake and makes up the largest part of the Mattamuskeet National Wildlife Refuge.

☛ The state's second largest lake is Lake Phelps covering about 16,600 acres. Although it's very large, it is also very shallow, with its deepest points between four and nine feet.

☛ Lake Waccamaw is another relatively shallow lake with an average depth of 7.5 feet. Scientists believe the lake is about 250,000 years old, and if you flew over it, you'd notice it's an almost perfect oval, measuring about five miles wide and seven miles long.

DID YOU  KNOW?

Scientists believe that the Black Mountains are more than one billion years old. There are many significant peaks within this region, and six of them are among the 10 highest peaks in the eastern part of the country. Mount Mitchell is one of those notable peaks and is the highest in the eastern U.S.

COUNTY CURIOSITIES

Forty-eight of the country's 50 states divide their geography into counties. On average, most states have 62 counties—North Carolina has a staggering 100. Each county is listed below, along with an interesting trivia tidbit.

Alamance

Alamance County had a large Quaker population during the American Revolution, and the outdoor drama *The Sword of Peace* highlights their life in Snow Camp during the summer. Textile magnate J. Spencer Love started Burlington Industries in the county in 1923 and dominated the textile market for much of the 20th century.

Alexander

The eight townships of Bethlehem, Ellendale, Gwaltney, Little River, Sugar Loaf, Taylorsville, Wittenburg and Stony Point make up the county of Alexander. Alexander is also home to the NAEM Mine—the mine that has unearthed the largest emeralds in North America.

Alleghany

The northwestern county of Alleghany borders Virginia, and it is completely located within the Appalachian Mountains region. Ranked as the fifth-smallest county, Alleghany only covers about 233 square miles.

Anson

The Huntley House is a large, white farmhouse located near the Anson County community of Lilesville, and it was the location for Steven Spielberg's blockbuster film *The Color Purple*. The county has drawn interest from other filmmakers as well—Marshville and other surrounding wooded areas were the setting for *The Evil Dead II*.

Ashe

The 427 square miles that make up Ashe County are located in the most northwesterly corner of North Carolina. The county is also home to New River State Park, and despite being called "New," the river is one of the oldest in the world.

Avery

Avery County is a relatively young county, with a centennial coming up in 2011. The 100th and final county added to the state, Avery takes its name from Colonel Waightstill Avery— North Carolina's first attorney general.

Beaufort

Beaufort County covers a total area of 959 square miles, and 131 square miles of that is covered in water. Bath, North Carolina's oldest incorporated town (founded in 1705), can be found here.

Bertie

Elevations in Bertie County, which is located in the Coastal Plain area of the state, range from 97 feet above sea level to sea level.

Bladen

Bladen County is surrounded by five counties: Cumberland to the north, Samson to the northeast, Pender to the southeast, Columbus to the south and Robeson to the west. Called the "Mother of Counties," 55 of North Carolina's 100 modern counties were created from Bladen's original land.

Brunswick

Brunswick County, the most southern county in the state, is home to the 1300-acre sanctuary called Bird Island. Until 2002, it was privately owned, but the state purchased the area for $4.2 million to use as a reserve.

Buncombe

Buncombe County is named after a Revolutionary War soldier, Colonel Edward Buncombe. Buncombe's surname was turned into a derogatory term in 1820 because of a misspelling—Bunkum. Have you ever heard the phrase, "That's a load of bunk"? Well, the word "bunkum" means senseless talk or nonsense. Just ask Felix Walker, the legislator from Buncombe County who, in 1820, created the reason for a reporter to intentionally misspell the name of the politician's home county.

Burke

Burke County was established on June 1, 1777, but the original county was considerably larger than its present configuration. That's because in 1834, the county was reduced to its current 514 square miles. The land taken away from Burke eventually became several other counties—Alexander, Buncombe, Caldwell, Catawba, Madison, Mitchell, McDowell and Yancey. Burke County's first courthouse was established in 1785 and constructed from what was most readily available at the time—logs.

Cabarrus

Cabarrus County calls itself "home to the number-one tourist destination in the state." That's because the town of Concord Mills, located in the southwestern part of North Carolina, boasts such major attractions as Lowe's Motor Speedway, the Reed Gold Mine and a plethora of beautiful parks. Racing legend Dale Earnhardt Sr. was born in Kannapolis, and a large number of NASCAR race teams are based in the county.

Caldwell

On January 11, 1841, Caldwell County was officially formed. A proposal for the new county was originally put to the state legislature in 1839 but was rejected. When a decision was finally made to go ahead with the new county, land was annexed from the two neighboring counties of Burke and Wilkes. The county was originally to be named Boone County, but the name Caldwell was chosen instead and honors Joseph Caldwell, the first president of the University of North Carolina in Chapel Hill.

Camden

Camden County's motto is "An Opportunity Awaits You." The county is what's known as a "consolidated city-county"—a county and city that have merged and formed a single government body. It's the only county in the state with this distinction. The state's oldest Baptist church, Shiloh Baptist, founded in 1729, is located here.

Carteret

Carteret County, the majority of which is located on the Atlantic Ocean, along what's called the Crystal Coast, boasts some of the best beaches in the state. Carteret County has only four neighboring counties: Craven and Pamlico to the north, Onslow to the west-southwest and Jones to the west-northwest.

Caswell

On the map, Caswell County looks like it forms a perfect square. It borders three Virginia counties to the north: Danville, Pittsylvania and Halifax. Person County borders it to the east, with Orange County on the southeast. Alamance County is located on Caswell's southwest border, and Rockingham is located along its western edge.

Catawba

Catawba County is home to the Hickory Museum of Art, the state's second oldest museum. The museum was founded by Paul Austin Wayne Whitener—a Hickory native and former

Duke University football player. It's housed in the Arts and Science Center of Catawba Valley.

Chatham

In the mid-1700s, several groups of settlers from Europe—including the Quakers—established communities in what would eventually become Chatham County. The county was officially established on April 1, 1771, but didn't appoint its first county manager until 1977. The Devil's Tramping Ground, a mysterious 40-foot circular area near Siler City where no vegetation will grow, can be found here as well.

DID YOU KNOW?

If you're into wild animals, you'll be interested to know that there are more Asian bearcats, also known as binturongs, housed at the Carnivore Preservation Trust, near Pittsboro, than there are in any other similar wildlife reserve in the country.

Cherokee

The most southwestern county in North Carolina is Cherokee County. Tennessee's Polk and Monroe counties to the west and northwest, respectively, the Georgia counties of Fannin in the south-southwest and Union in the south-southeast border the 497 square miles that make up Cherokee County, along with the three North Carolina counties of Graham to the northeast, Macon to the east and Clay to the southeast.

Chowan

North Carolina's oldest county, Albemarle County, was established in 1664 but no longer exists. In 1668, it was reorganized into the four counties of Chowan, Currituck, Pasquotank and Perquimans, making these four counties the oldest in the state.

Clay

Clay County was formed in February 1861, but a county government wasn't created until 1868. The county was named for Kentucky presidential candidate Henry Clay. You can find Jack Rabbit and Chunky Gal mountains in the county.

Cleveland

Cleveland County calls itself the "gateway between Asheville and Charlotte." It is home to an estimated 98,932 people. The average age of Cleveland's residents is 39.

Cumberland

There are nine municipalities occupying the 661 square miles that make up Cumberland County. One of those municipalities—Fayetteville—is the county seat and home to Fort Bragg, one of the largest military institutions in the United States.

Currituck

Currituck County takes its name from the Algonquian language. "Currituck" means "the land of the wild goose."

Dare

Dare County was named after a baby girl. Born on August 18, 1587, Virginia Dare was the first non-Native child born in the county, as well as the new land we like to call America. Dare County is also the largest county in North Carolina, covering 1562 square miles.

Davidson

Davidson County is the 11th largest county in North Carolina. It is also home to the world's largest Duncan Phyfe chair (Thomasville) and to the Barbecue Capital of the World (Lexington).

Davie
There are 34,835 people living in the 267 square miles that make up Davie County, giving it a density of about 132 people per square mile. One of North Carolina's oldest festivals—the Mocksville Masonic Picnic—has been held here every August since 1878.

Duplin
Number crunchers suggest the population of Duplin County has grown steadily from its 2000 census population figure of 49,000 to a current population of an estimated 53,000.
The Duplin Winery (creative name, I know), the oldest winery in the state, was founded here in the 1960s.

Durham
Durham County is 16 miles long and 25 miles wide, giving it an area of only 400 square miles. It is home to just one city, which is also named Durham. Durham County is part of the Triangle area, which also includes Wake and Orange counties.

Edgecombe
Edgecombe County first established its boundaries in 1741, but at that time, it was considerably larger than the 507 square miles it covers today. That's because, over the years, parts of the original county were annexed to form other counties: Granville in 1746, Halifax in 1758, Nash in 1777 and part of Wilson in 1855.

Forsyth
A Carver High School student named Willie H. Johnson Jr. designed Forsyth County's official seal. He created the seal in 1949 and submitted it to a contest being held as part of the county's centennial celebrations. Krispy Kreme doughnuts and the Wachovia Banking corporation both got their starts in Forsyth, which is also the home of Wake Forest University. "Oh here's to Wake Forest, a glass of the finest…"

Franklin

Louisburg College, founded in 1787, is the nation's oldest two-year institution and is located in Franklin County. In case you hadn't guessed, the county was named after Benjamin Franklin.

Gaston

The first European residents of what is now Gaston County were the Scots, the Irish, the English and the Pennsylvania Dutch. In 1870, Gaston was known as the "Banner Corn Whiskey County of Carolina."

Gates

In 1790, the population of Gates County was 5372. Over the years, the county has grown, albeit slowly. In 2002, the county's population was an estimated 10,720, giving it a friendly, small-town feel.

Graham

Graham County calls itself "North Carolina's last frontier." That's because most of the 302 square miles it covers are still forested, and much of that forest is virgin timber. It's also a dry county, just so you know…

Granville

The area now called Granville County was once home to the Tuscarora Indians. Europeans first settled in the area around 1711, and the county was officially formed in 1746.

Greene

Snow Hill, Greene County's largest commercial center, is also the county seat. An outsider might wonder if it actually snows all that much in Snow Hill, but the name didn't come from the white, fluffy flakes of northern winters. Instead, the county was named for the white, sandy shores of Contentnea Creek.

Guilford

Guilford County covers 649 square miles and was established in 1771. Its estimated population, as of 2007, was 465,931, and folks living in Guilford earn an average of $38,900.

Halifax

In early November, North Carolina's cotton fields are in full bloom, and a drive through Halifax County is nothing if not breathtaking at this time of the year. The Halifax Resolves, the first uprising for independence from Great Britain, was passed here on April 12, 1776. Don't believe me? Check the NC state flag; it's one of the two dates on it.

Harnett

Harnett County was founded in 1855 and named after Cornelius Harnett, a merchant, farmer and statesman who was a leader in the Revolutionary War. He went on to become a delegate for North Carolina in the Continental Congress from 1777 to 1779. My alma mater, Campbell University, is located here in the town of Buies Creek.

Haywood

Folks living in or visiting Haywood County will likely experience moderate temperatures, with an average of about 38°F in January and an average temperature of around 71°F in June. Haywood County has one of the highest elevations of any county, at a mean of 3600 feet.

Henderson

Of Henderson County's 375 square miles, only one square mile is covered in water. Also, the county leads the state in apple production.

Hertford

According to U.S. census estimates from 2008, the racial makeup of Hertford County is as follows: 35.9 percent white, 61.6 percent black or African American, 1.2 percent American Indian and Alaska Native, and 0.5 percent Asian. There was 34.6 percent of the population that reported being white but not Hispanic, 2.1 percent reported being of Hispanic or Latino origin and 0.8 percent reported being of two or more races.

Hoke

Hoke County was formed in 1911. Its county seat is Raeford. The county also hosts the North Carolina Turkey Festival, honoring the fact that the Tar Heel State leads the nation in turkey production.

Hyde

Hyde County is North Carolina's slowest growing county. In fact, based on figures from 2000 and estimates from 2003, the population actually decreased by 4.4 percent, from 5826 to 5567, respectively.

Iredell

The elevation of Iredell County ranges from 700 to 1760 feet above sea level. The largest artificial lake in the state, Lake Norman, has over 520 miles of shoreline inside the county. Also, the North Carolina Racing Hall of Fame and Race City USA are located in Mooresville—along with several NASCAR Sprint Cup team headquarters.

Jackson

Jackson County was named in honor of Andrew Jackson, the seventh president of the United States. The county was founded in 1851 and, for a time, the community of Webster served as the county seat. That changed in 1913, when Sylva took over that responsibility.

Johnston

The largest Civil War battle fought in North Carolina was the Battle of Bentonville. It took place from March 19 to 21, 1865, near the community of Four Oaks, in eastern Johnston County. I've seen the battle's reenactment. It was pretty cool, right up to the field hospital where fake limbs were tossed through a window onto a big pile.

Jones

Jones County's official website points out that there are very few traffic lights in the county. In some locations, that could pose a few problems, but folks at the county office report "no traffic congestion" for them!

Lee

There's a lot to see in Lee County, but one of the most unique attractions is the Endor Iron Furnace near Cumnock. This pig-iron furnace, which is located on a 426-acre property, was operational until 1874. Plans are underway to develop the site into a nature preserve and restore the furnace to its original glory.

Lenoir

Lenoir County occupies an even 400 square miles of land, with about 149.2 residents per square mile based on 2000 census figures. Population estimates from 2004 suggest that there are more females in the county than males, with the fairer sex making up about 52.6 percent of the population.

Lincoln

Lincoln County is located in the western third of North Carolina and was founded in 1779. According to its official county website, there are 23 other Lincoln counties in the country. Unlike some of the others, whose founding fathers chose the name in honor of Abraham Lincoln, North Carolina's Lincoln County was named after the American Revolutionary War general, Benjamin Lincoln.

Macon
Mining forms a large part of Macon County's economy, and the county seat of Franklin calls itself the "gem capital of the world." Semi-precious stones and precious gems such as sapphires and rubies are harvested in some of the area's mines.

Madison
Madison County is named after former president, James Madison, our fourth president, who served from 1809 to 1817. The county was formed in 1851.

Martin
According to information collected by the U.S. Census Bureau from 2006 to 2008, men out-earned women in Martin County by a significant margin. The median earnings for a full-time, year-round male worker were an estimated $35,503, while a woman in the same category earned only $23,617.

McDowell
With a motto like "Great History, Exciting Future," it's a sure bet that folks living in McDowell County are a positive-thinking bunch. The Scots-Irish were the first Europeans to settle in the area in the early 1700s, but human inhabitation here dates back 6000 years to when the first Native Americans lived in the area.

Mecklenburg
Mecklenburg County takes its name from the German state of Mecklenburg-Strelitz. Eight of the Fortune 500 companies named each year in the U.S. are headquartered here.

Mitchell

Mitchell County was named after an educator. Elisha Mitchell was a professor at the University of North Carolina, where he taught mathematics, chemistry, mineralogy and geology from 1818 until his death in 1857.

Montgomery

The average annual rainfall in Montgomery County is 47 inches, which helps the Uwharrie National Forest, a wilderness area that represents much of the region's character.

Moore

Moore County, founded in 1783, was named after Alfred Moore, an officer who served in the American Revolutionary War. The tourism industry is big for Moore County, seeing as how it is home to the Pinehurst Golf Club—and the world-famous No. 2 course. Let's tee it up!

Nash

About one-third of Nash County's annual operating budget is spent on county schools and the approximately 21,000 students who attend those institutions.

New Hanover

Folks in New Hanover County appear to be evenly split when it comes to their political allegiances, voting in both Democrats and Republicans fairly equally over the years and during different elections.

Northampton

There are about 22,086 people living in Northampton County. The community of Jackson serves as its county seat. Most of Northampton County is within a one-day drive of 40 percent of the American population because it sits near the middle of the Atlantic Seaboard. Northampton also had a very active thoroughbred horseracing scene—well before its Kentucky counterpart—in the early 19th century.

Onslow

The city of Jacksonville, named in honor of President Andrew Jackson, serves as the Onslow County seat. Parts of the Carteret and New Hanover colonial precincts were annexed to form this county in 1734. Jacksonville is also one of America's principal military cities, thanks in part to Camp Lejeune Marine Base.

Orange

Five different American Indian tribes—including the Eno, Haw and the Occaneechi—were living in the area now known as Orange County when the first European settlers arrived in 1752. The county got its name from William V of Orange, the grandson of King George III of England.

Pamlico

One of Pamlico County's most striking geographic features is its abundance of water. Just over 40 percent of its total 364,400-acre area, or 151,000 acres, is covered in water, and the remaining 213,400 acres are land. It's no surprise that the county's largest industries are natural-resource based. The area's first inhabitants were the Pampticoe Indians. Inspired by the area's natural beauty, they called the area TaTaku, which means "where the land and sea meet the sky."

Pasquotank

Pasquotank County gets its name from the Algonquian word *pasketanki*. Generally speaking, the word means "where the current of the stream divides or forks." The county was formed in 1668 and today covers a land area of just under 227 square miles.

Pender

The first southern battle of the Revolutionary War—the Battle of Moore's Creek Bridge—took place on February 27, 1776, in what is now Pender County. Residents of the county are proud of its beautiful, natural landscapes and moderate climate, and these attributes seem to attract newcomers as well. Since 1990, the county's population has increased by 15 percent!

Perquimans

Perquimans (*per-QUIM-ans*) County is bordered on the east by Pasquotank County, on the southeast by the Atlantic Ocean (100 miles of shoreline), on the southwest by Chowan County, and on the northwest by Gates County. Hall of Fame baseball player Jim "Catfish" Hunter called Perquimans home, specifically the town of Hertford.

Person

A population of 37,341 individuals comprises 14,085 households and 10,113 families in Person County. The county was named for General Thomas Person, a Revolutionary War patriot who made significant contributions to Person County and surrounding areas. A trustee of the University of North Carolina-Chapel Hill, General Person donated large sums of money to the institution, and Person Hall was built in his honor. The county also hosts the Person-ality Festival every year. That's just a way cool name for a festival

Pitt

There are 10 municipalities that make up Pitt County. The smallest municipality, population-wise, is Falkland. It is home to just 112 people. Greenville, the county seat, is home to East Carolina University—where my sister-in-law graduated. Go Pirates!

Polk

Polk County is located in the western portion of North Carolina, with two thirds of the county located on the Piedmont and the westernmost third of the county hugging the Blue Ridge Mountains. Elevation levels in Polk County range from 800 feet to the 3200-foot summit of Tryon Peak.

Randolph

Randolph County has a couple of the biggest and best claims. It's home to the NC Zoo, the country's largest natural-habitat zoo. And because it neighbors Chatham County, North Carolina's geographic center, to the east, Randolph County describes itself as being the "heart of North Carolina."

Richmond

Richmond County was founded in 1779 and named in honor of Charles Lennox, the 3rd Duke of Richmond. The county seat, Rockingham, is home to the North Carolina Motor Speedway, locally known as "The Rock." The last race at the Rock was in February 2004, and I was in attendance. It was definitely bittersweet.

Robeson

Robeson County is divided into 29 townships, and Lumberton is its county seat. The Lumbee Indians are a big part of Robeson history. Two of the ways Robeson celebrates its Native American heritage are with the Lumbee Spring Powwow and the Native American Big Game Festival.

Rockingham

An estimated 91,928 people call Rockingham County home, making it the 25th most populated county in the state. Rockingham got its name from Charles Watson-Wentworth, the 2nd Marquis of Rockingham, and was formed in 1785.

The county seat, Wentworth, shares the same namesake and was incorporated in 1799.

Rowan

Anyone wanting to learn about Rowan County, or western North Carolina in general, need only visit the Edith M. Clark History Room. Located in the Rowan Public Library, the reading room is named in honor of Edith Montcalm Clark, the woman who served as the library's director for almost 36 years. The History Room contains more than 19,000 books, 5700 microforms, 268 manuscript collections, dozens of genealogical journals and a solid collection of Civil War military and prison materials. In a word, the room is priceless.

Rutherford

Rutherford County's motto is "A County for All Seasons." The moderate climate and atmosphere make this county a pleasant place to live, work and raise children year round. Filmmaking has also been a boon to the Rutherford economy, with parts of the movies *Last of the Mohicans* (1992), *Dirty Dancing* (1987) and *Firestarter* (1984) filmed in the county.

Sampson

Sampson County was carved out of Duplin County in 1784. It was named in honor of John Sampson, Duplin County's first "Register of Deeds." Sampson went on to become the first mayor of Wilmington, the county seat of New Hanover.

Scotland

The entire 321 square miles that make up Scotland County were taken from neighboring Richmond County. Scotland County was founded on February 20, 1899, making it one of the state's youngest counties.

Stanly

The per capita income in Stanly County is $17,825, based on 2000 census figures. Just over eight percent of families and almost 11 percent of the entire population of Stanly live below the poverty line.

Stokes

One of the most interesting bits of history from Stokes County was discovered in 1972, when 25 separate American Indian burial sites were discovered. The area is referred to as the Saura, after the Saura people who once inhabited the area near Walnut Cove.

Surry

Surry County boasts at least 18 significant peaks ranging in elevation from Stott Knob at 1552 feet to Surry's highest summit, Fisher Peak, at 3570 feet. You can also find *Andy Griffith Show* memorabilia in Surry, such as Snappy Lunch, Floyd's City Barber Shop and the Andy Griffith Playhouse.

Swain

Mountain peaks make up a considerable portion of Swain County, which is predominantly situated within Great Smoky Mountains National Park. The highest peak in the county is Clingmans Dome, with an elevation of 6643 feet. Tourism is the main source of income for the county, which is also home to the Qualla Boundary—the reservation for the Eastern Band of Cherokee Indians.

Transylvania

There are 250 waterfalls throughout Transylvania County, giving it the reputation for being the "Land of Waterfalls." At a height of 411 feet, Whitewater Falls is not only the highest waterfall in the county, but no other waterfall east of the Rocky Mountains is higher.

Tyrrell

Tyrrell is the state's least populous county, and according to 2008 census estimates, approximately 4087 people live here. Of that number, 43.8 percent are female, and 5.6 percent are less than five years old. The town of Frying Pan Landing is in Tyrrell County.

Union

Union County prides itself on being one of the fastest growing counties in North Carolina. In 2000, the U.S. Census reported the county's population at 123,677. By 2008, the population had ballooned to an estimated 193,255.

 The state's top three fastest growing counties are Union, Currituck and Camden. Based on figures from 2000 and estimates from 2003, Union County's population increased by 18 percent, giving it the largest growth margin. Currituck and Camden were in second place with 14.5 and 14.2 percent growth, respectively.

Vance
The land that makes up Vance County was once part of the State of Virginia. England's King Charles II revamped the boundaries between Carolina and Virginia in 1665, putting what would eventually become Vance County into Carolina.

Wake
If the folks down at Fishing Works are right, Wake County offers anglers with the largest variety of fishing holes. There are about 123 "fishing lakes" in the county. Wake County is also home to Raleigh, North Carolina's capital city, and to North Carolina State University.

Warren

Formed in 1779, Warren County has been the birthplace of many of North Carolina's most famous political leaders, such as former U.S. Senator and Speaker of the U.S. House of Representatives Nathaniel Macon (1757–1837). That being said, voters in Warren County typically vote for the Democratic Party.

Washington

Washington County is home to one of the state's last virgin forests, which is located in Pettigrew State Park. Named for President George Washington, the county was formed in 1799 from the western third of Tyrrell County.

Watauga

Watauga County is entirely located within the Appalachian Mountains. Because of its high elevation, the county is considerably cooler than neighboring areas during the summer and winter months.

Wayne

There's no record of European settlers or other explorers venturing into the area now known as Wayne County prior to 1730. The county was founded on November 2, 1779, and was named for Revolutionary War general "Mad Anthony" Wayne. The Mt. Olive Pickle Company can also be found here and produces the second-best-selling brand of pickled cucumbers in the nation.

Wilkes

One of Wilkes County's tourist draws, at least when it comes to music lovers, is the Hometown Opry, which offers weekly performances of traditional mountain music. In fact, according to Ted Lehmann, bluegrass lover and blogger, Wilkes County is an ongoing "hotbed of roots music."

Wilson

The economy of Wilson County is supported by the agricultural, automobile and pharmaceutical industries. Wilson is also known for its pork barbecue, including Bill Ellis and his world famous BBQ restaurant. Some residents of the county pronounce Wilson a little differently than most, adding a "T" into the county name so it sounds like "Wiltson."

Yadkin

In 1673, James Needham and Gabriel Arthur traveled through what would eventually become Yadkin County on a fact-finding mission for their employer, trader Abraham Wood. Wood wanted them to investigate trading opportunities with the Native American tribes in the area. The name Yadkin comes from the Siouan language, but there's no clear definition of the word. Some theories suggest that it means "big tree" or "place of big trees."

Yancey

Yancey County is one of two counties in the state that forbids the sale of alcohol. The other dry county is Graham. Yancey is home to Mount Mitchell, the tallest mountain in the state (6684 feet) and the highest peak east of the Mississippi River.

AVERAGES AND EXTREMES

Generally Speaking

Despite the fluctuations in temperatures and precipitation levels created by a varied topography, the climate of North Carolina is one of its attractions. Typically, it's never extremely cold, even in winter, and, aside from the Appalachians, which are categorized as having a "subtropical highland climate," summers throughout the rest of the state are characterized by warm, humid, subtropical conditions. Summer daytime temperatures are often around 90°F. In the winter, residents can expect temperatures to hover around 50°F.

All-Time High

The mercury hit 110°F in Fayetteville on August 21, 1983. This is the highest temperature ever officially recorded in the state.

All-Time Low

The lowest temperature on the books in North Carolina is –34°F. That record was set on Mount Mitchell, on January 21, 1985.

Middle of the Road

North Carolina's average high temperature is 88.3°F. The state's average low temperature is 27.3°F. However, in reality, average temperatures vary considerably between the state's higher elevations and the lower, coastal areas. For example, winter temperatures in the mountainous parts of North Carolina can routinely drop to 0°F, which is much colder than in the Piedmont and coastal areas of the state.

The Wet-and-Dry Cycle

North Carolina doesn't usually distinguish between wet and dry seasons. The rain falls when it does, but July usually sees the most rainfall. Again, geography has a lot to do with the amount of precipitation that is normal or average in any given area. For example, it's not uncommon to have an annual average of 90 inches of rain in the southwestern portion of the state. Here are a few precipitation averages:

☛ The Piedmont usually gets between 44 and 48 inches of rain in a year.

☛ The Coastal Plain typically sees between 44 and 56 inches of rain per year.

☛ Average annual snowfall across the state varies from just one inch in the Outer Banks and along the lower coast to about 10 inches in the northern Piedmont and 16 inches in the southern mountains.

☛ Mount Mitchell, the area of the state that gets the highest annual snowfall, gets an average of 50 inches of snow each winter.

☛ The Cape Hatteras National Seashore is quite lucky to see a dusting of snow in any given year.

☛ The North Carolina State Climate Office has identified the valley of the French Broad River as the driest point south of Virginia and east of the Mississippi River. Average annual precipitation in this area is somewhere around 37 inches.

Stormy Weather

As a coastal state, North Carolina is no stranger to extreme weather conditions. From high winds that develop into tornadoes and tropical cyclones to thunderstorms and hurricanes, residents who call this state home need to be prepared for just about anything.

☛ In 1974, Cyclone Tracy tore through a 30-mile area between Raleigh and Chapel Hill. The North Carolina State Climate Office lists Cyclone Tracy as the smallest storm to hit the state.

☛ The largest storm recorded in North Carolina was Typhoon Tip. In 1970, the typhoon ripped through a wide patch of land measuring 1400 miles in diameter.

☛ In March 1984, a series of tornadoes did as much damage as any hurricane could. Sixty-one people were killed, more than 1000 were injured and more than $120 million in damages were recorded.

DID YOU KNOW?

Based on the tables established by the Climate Office of North Carolina, it appears the practice of naming storms didn't occur until 1952, when Tropical Storm Abel made an appearance. This storm did not make landfall in North Carolina. The first storm to make landfall and be given a name was Hurricane Barbara in 1953.

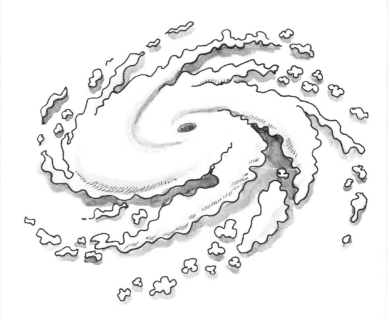

Hurricane Season

A storm reaches hurricane status when the winds of a tropical storm hit or surpass 74 miles per hour. Coastal communities along the country's Eastern Seaboard need to prepare for the possibility of hurricanes from June 1 to the end of November, with September typically seeing the most and deadliest storms. That said, North Carolina has been hit by lethal tropical storms outside the typical hurricane season. Here is some interesting, if not frightening, trivia on North Carolina's most severe weather conditions:

☛ A surprise hit the North Carolina coastline in early May 2007. That's when an out-of-season tropical storm named Andrea reached the coast.

☛ North Carolina can expect to be hit by a tropical cyclone about once every four years.

☛ The state's most vulnerable areas are Cape Hatteras, Cape Fear and Cape Lookout. If a storm makes landfall, these are often the locations where that will happen.

☛ Based on the tables established by the State Climate Office, it appears that the practice of naming storms didn't begin until 1952, when Tropical Storm Abel made an appearance. This storm did not make landfall in North Carolina. The first storm to make landfall and be given a name was Hurricane Barbara in 1953.

☛ About 50 storms have made landfall in North Carolina since the mid-1800s, when weather records started to be kept.

☛ In 1984, the Category 4 Hurricane Diane caused $36 million in damages when it hit North Carolina's coast.

☛ An unnamed hurricane in 1857 was likely the state's deadliest, killing 424 people.

☛ Hurricane Fran in 1996 prompted North Carolinians to get buttons that said, "I Survived Fran." The eye of the hurricane crossed directly over Raleigh, some two hours inland. I slept through it, scary enough.

☛ Hurricane Floyd caused 35 deaths and flooded much of North Carolina's east coast. The 1999 hurricane was the deadliest in recent history.

☞ North Carolina is listed as the fourth most popular state when it comes to attracting hurricane landfall, with a total of 50 reported since 1851.

☞ There has never been a Category 5 hurricane, defined as "devastating" with winds of more than 155 miles per hour, to hit North Carolina. The state's most damaging hurricanes have been Category 3 or "strong," but there have been a few Category 4 or "very strong" hurricanes. The most recent Category 4 storm was Hurricane Charley in 2004.

 Severe storms can alter geography! Oregon Inlet and Hatteras Inlet were created by a hurricane in September 1846.

DID YOU KNOW?

North Carolina's only professional hockey team took the name Carolina Hurricanes when the NHL's Hartford Whalers moved to Raleigh in 1997. Their mascot is a pig named Stormy, and the cheerleaders are called the Storm Squad. Why is the mascot a pig? It's because of North Carolina's love of pork barbecue.

ANIMALS

North Carolina's wildlife is as varied and beautiful as the state's geography, but if you check out the NC Wildlife Resources Commission, there are an awful lot of species that scientists are concerned about. Fifty-eight species of birds, mammals, fish or amphibians are currently listed as "endangered," which means that the species' continued existence in the state is in jeopardy. Another 51 species are currently listed as "threatened"—without conservation efforts these species will become endangered in the near future. Another 129 species are being carefully monitored and listed as being of "special concern."

It's Lovely Being Green

The southern leopard frog, or one of its closely related cousins, can be found in all of the Lower 48 states. Found throughout North Carolina, this amphibian is considered the most common frog in the Coastal Plain.

DID YOU KNOW?

Great Smoky Mountains National Park is known as the "Salamander Capital of the World," but one specimen is found only in the Tar Heel State. The Neuse River waterdog (*Necturus lewisi*) can be found along the banks of one of the state's biggest and most important rivers.

There is a herd of about 100 wild horses that still lives near Shackleford Banks, which is part of the Outer Banks coastal system.

Chicken or Egg?

There would be no domestic pigs were it not for the wild boar. Hampshire pigs and Russian boars are the two types of wild boar found in the country, but they're usually crossbred with domestic pigs. The North Carolina Wildlife Resources Commission in Cherokee, Clay, Graham, Jackson, Macon and Swain counties only recognizes wild boar. Other counties consider wild boars to be "feral hogs."

White-tailed Wonder

The white-tailed deer is one of five deer species common to North America, but it is the most prevalent species in North Carolina. The North Carolina Wildlife Resources Commission estimates that there are about 1.25 million white-tailed deer in the state.

Barking Dog

North Carolina coyotes are smaller and have pointed ears and long snouts, but otherwise they look remarkably similar to red wolves. These creatures are marvelous at adapting to their surroundings, and with the decline in the grey wolf, the coyote has prospered in all 100 counties. The name "coyote" comes from the Aztec word *coyotl,* which means "barking dog."

Cute as a Button
The southern flying squirrel is found throughout the state, regardless of issues of habitat and geography. Although there are about 33 species of flying squirrels, the southern flying squirrel, the most common variety in North Carolina, is one of only two flying squirrel species found in the state—the other is the northern flying squirrel.

Keeper of Dreams
The only bear common to North Carolina and the western United States is the black bear. The average life expectancy of the black bear is between four and five years, but a few have been known to survive much longer. A Cherokee legend refers to the black bear as "the keeper of dreams."

DID YOU  KNOW?

The most photographed black bear in North Carolina history was the legendary Mildred, brought to Grandfather Mountain in 1967 by Hugh Morton. Even though she died in 1993 at the very old age of 26, Mildred will forever be considered a symbol of the High Country. She was "the bear that didn't know she was a bear."

Fancy Fur

Muskrats are found throughout North Carolina and are legally trapped, most commonly for their fur. There was a time, however, when the population of muskrats was rapidly declining. From the 1940s to the 1960s, biologist Kenneth A. Wilson studied the issue and came up with several strategies on how to better manage the muskrat and protect its habitat. Today, there are sufficient numbers that hunting and regularly culling their numbers has become a maintenance issue.

Handsome Haul

The raccoon is another abundant furbearer living in the state. There are at least six (and some say seven) raccoon species wandering throughout North, Central and South America, but *Procyon lotor*, the common raccoon, is the only one you'll find in the North Carolina countryside. The North Carolina Wildlife Resources Commission calls the ring-tailed critter one of the state's "most economically important furbearers," a claim that extends to most of the country as well.

Tread Carefully

Anyone who sees this furry critter doesn't usually stick around to make friends. Full grown, the striped skunk is comparable in size to a house cat. The striped skunk is common throughout most of North Carolina, except for a small portion of the southeastern part of the state.

Bushy-tailed Rodents

The fox squirrel is the largest and most colorful tree squirrel in the state. It is most commonly found in the eastern portion and in the remote, northwest corner of the state. Although the number of fox squirrels living in North Carolina has declined, this squirrel is still considered a game species.

Not Just Dangerous, But Deadly

Six of the 37 varieties of snakes found in North Carolina are venomous. For people who are not snake lovers, the creature doesn't have to be deadly for them to keep their distance. Still, it's not a bad idea to at least know which of these slithering serpents are more dangerous than the others:

☛ The eastern coral snake is a distant relative of India's deadly cobras. Need I say more? Mostly nocturnal, it is black and deep red, with thin, yellow bands separating each color. This snake is considered rare, inhabits the southernmost tip of the state and is the deadliest venomous snake in North Carolina. On the upside, this snake is also people-shy, and encounters are extremely rare.

☛ Copperhead and canebrake rattlesnakes are found throughout the state. Copperheads prefer to live in the forest and hide under stones, stumps and abandoned woodpiles. The cane-brake rattlesnake prefers fields and hills, and lives along the edges of the forests.

☛ Eastern diamondback and pigmy rattlesnakes are found primarily in the southeastern part of the state. Rattlesnakes can see equally well in the day or night, and they birth youngsters who are fully equipped to protect themselves with venom that's even more potent than that of an adult rattler.

☛ The cottonmouth or water moccasin is found primarily in the eastern portion of the state. Officials warn people to stay away from the cottonmouth at all costs, as its bite can be fatal.

Slithery Creature

For those folks who are so inclined, North Carolina's corn snake is said to make a lovely pet. It's easily recognized, with red, orange, gray and brown coloring, and it's said to have a "docile" temperament. The corn snake can be found in southern parts of the state. While most corn snakes die young, some kept in captivity have lived into their third decade. I actually own a corn snake, and her name is Cocoa Pop. I won't tell you what happened to Shimmy, our first corn snake.

DID YOU KNOW?

There are several spiders in North Carolina that, if they bite, could cause injury and discomfort. Among these species is the black widow spider. Although both males and females of the species inject venom when they bite, a bite received from an adult female black widow spider is usually more severe and often requires the administration of an antivenin serum.

Another nasty little spider that is barely as large as a quarter is the brown recluse. If it bites, the wound will turn red, and the surrounding flesh can become necrotic.

FEATHERED FRIENDS

Bird Stew

Quail, also known as partridge, was a common staple for early settlers in the state. Over the years, quail numbers have greatly diminished, mostly because of habitat loss. Natural predators have also assisted in this decline, as have avid hunters.

Bobwhite quail can live to the age of five years, but about 80 percent die before their first birthday. Quail season runs from October to February.

Here and Gone Again

Mourning doves are transient birds with a range that extends from Alaska to Panama. Because they're also birds that like continuity, populations of mourning doves that have at one time settled in North Carolina often return year after year. The largest flocks tend to gather in August and September, when migratory birds augment local populations. Those colonies of birds that nest and raise their young in North Carolina normally pair up by February. Egg laying begins in March and can continue into September. Populations of mourning doves in North Carolina are sparsest in October and November.

DID YOU  KNOW?

Sylvan Heights Waterfowl Park, located in the small eastern town of Scotland Neck, is the world's largest waterfowl park and eco-reserve. The park provides zoos all over the world with an amazing variety of birds.

Everybody Knows This Name

The green head and yellow beak of the male mallard duck are so familiar that even very young children know its name. The mallard's ability to adapt to a variety of habitats is a big reason why it's considered the most abundant and commonly recognized species of duck in North America. It's not uncommon for mallards to nest in North Carolina, and this duck is fair game to hunters across the continent. In 2007, there were an estimated 8.5 million mallards in North America.

White Beauty

The snowy egret is commonly referred to as North Carolina's most charming marsh bird and can be seen along the coastal areas of the state. At one time, the bird's long, white feathers were in high demand by the state's milliners. Egrets were often shot during nesting season, when they were easy targets, and this resulted in a seriously depleted population. The damage was so extensive that in 1898, T. Gilbert Pearson, an ornithologist, couldn't find a single breeding pair of snowy egrets anywhere along the coast. Pearson highlighted the plight of the species to the National Association of Audubon Societies, and public awareness went a long way in restoring and maintaining the presence of this species in North Carolina. It is still listed as a species of special concern.

Sea Hawks of the Water

With a length of as much as 24 inches and a potential wingspan of 72 inches, an osprey is easy to indentify if you encounter one. This is especially true if you're around when the bird spots a fish and plummets, at speeds of between 30 and 50 miles per hour, into the water. Ospreys have sharp, spiny projections on the pads of their feet that make these raptors particularly adept at catching and holding on to their slimy prey.

The osprey is another example of a situation in which public awareness saved a species from potential extinction. The use of DDT and other pesticides resulted in a severe depletion of North Carolina's osprey population during the 1960s. When the use of these "persistent pesticides" was banned in the mid-1970s, osprey populations bounced back and the species is once again a regular inhabitant of the state. Some folks call the osprey the "sea hawk of the water."

Large and In Charge
Noted ornithologist T. Gilbert Pearson once described the great horned owl as "the feathered tiger of the air." This species is the largest owl in the state and is found throughout North Carolina. The great horned owl has brilliant yellow eyes, feeds on rodents and smaller birds and likes to hoot when it's looking for love. Both federal and state laws prohibit anyone from hurting, harassing or killing these owls—or any other bird of prey for that matter.

HERE FISHY, FISHY

Spicy Delicacy

Within North Carolina's boundaries, there are an estimated 40 varieties of the mini-lobster look-alikes called crayfish. Two of these species are unique to the state: *Cambarus catagius,* or the Greensboro burrowing crayfish, is found only in the Greensboro area, and *Orconectes carolinensis,* or the North Carolina spiny crayfish, is found only in the Tar and Neuse river basins in the Coastal Plain. Crayfish are a large part of traditional North Carolina and Southern cuisine.

Angler's Delight

Most avid fishermen are thrilled with every pull on the plug, but by far the most popular species of fish in North Carolina, and the entire country for that matter, is the largemouth bass. This game fish is found throughout the state but occurs in greater numbers in the Piedmont and the Coastal Plain.

Home Grown

The bluegill is one of North Carolina's native fish species and is found in every county. A member of the sunfish family, the bluegill is related to the largemouth bass. Although a typical lifespan for the bluegill is around four years, some 10-year-old specimens have been recorded.

Favorite Fish

There are two species of crappie native to North Carolina—the papermouth and the speckled perch. Although they're much smaller than some species of fish, crappies are still angler favorites. They are also thought to be the best tasting!

It's in the Name

The tangerine darter's scientific name is *Percina aurantiaca*, which means "small, orange-colored perch." This species is native to North Carolina but is limited to the mountainous western region of the state. The tangerine darter is a non-game species.

Rare Find

The Roanoke hogsucker is another non-game fish most frequently found in parts of the Roanoke River. Although this variety of sucker is native to North Carolina, its numbers are decreasing and the North Carolina Natural Heritage Program lists it as "significantly rare." While this hogsucker isn't caught to eat, anglers don't mind snagging one now and again because the fish is quite the challenge to reel in.

Also Known As

The Carolina madtom is related to bullheads and catfish. This particular species, which is the only madtom natural to North Carolina, is smaller than its cousins, growing to a maximum of five inches in length. It's most commonly found in North Carolina's Tar and Neuse river basins.

I Heard That!

The American shad is primarily found in waterways in the eastern portion of the state. It's a member of the herring family, and, in an effort to replenish rapidly depleting stocks, the North Carolina Wildlife Resources Commission and the U.S. Fish and Wildlife Service stocked the Roanoke River with more than eight million fry.

Ocean Lovers

The Atlantic sturgeon is one of the most unique looking of North Carolina's fish, with barbels and bony plates that give it an almost prehistoric appearance. The sturgeon can grow to a length of nine feet, weigh as much as 500 pounds and live to the age of 60. This species is primarily found along North Carolina's coastal areas.

Prized Pick

The walleye, a member of the perch family, is another angler's favorite, fitting into the category of best-tasting freshwater fish. Historically, the walleye was believed to inhabit the lower Pigeon and French Broad rivers, but the species generally prefers quiet waters and is more common in lakes and reservoirs in the southeastern part of the state and along the northern border.

PLANT LIFE

Some Like It Wet!
The wide variety of plant life in North Carolina is extensive, but while some plants can adapt to a variety of weather and soil conditions, others have their preferences. When it comes to the wetlands, there are a few plants that are found in this habitat 99 percent of the time:

- The water tupelo can grow to a height of over 90 feet, with small clusters of blue-black fruits growing near its large leaves.

- The Atlantic white-cedar is another wetland lover, bearing small cones and flattened leaves.

- The bald cypress has a cone-shaped crown until it gets old, then it "balds" like an aging man and develops a flat top.

- The black willow is short in stature, around 50 feet in height, with willowy leaves that grow to a length of five inches.

- The buttonbush is a small shrub that, grows to between three and 10 feet tall. It likes to live along the shores of lakes and ponds.

- The daisy-like sea ox-eye grows in colonies and prefers brackish and salt marshes.

- The swamp rose boasts the large, pink flowers, prickly thorns and red rose hips of any other rosebush—this one just prefers to grow near water.

- The arrow arum is aptly named. This herb boasts long, broad, triangular leaves that look like arrowheads.

- The arrowhead, or duck potato, also sports leaves that look similar to arrowheads. This herb blooms white flowers.

☛ The Asiatic dayflower is a trailing herb with blue flowers. Although lovely, it is an invasive, non-native plant.

☛ The southern blue flag is a member of the iris family and is quite easily identified by its blue-purple flower.

☛ Most everyone is familiar with the common or broad-leaved cattail, a perennial herb that grows up to 10 feet in height and sports a brown bulrush. This particular species has broader leaves than the narrow-leaved cattail.

☛ The netted chainfern grows to a maximum height of 1.5 feet and prefers to live in acidic swamps and wet pine woods.

☛ The royal fern is a wetland herb that prefers swamps and marshes. It is common throughout the state.

☛ The Virginia chainfern thrives in wet soils, but it flourishes in the sun.

☛ Apparently, if you were to chew on perennial glasswort you'd notice that the plant has a salty taste, likely because it thrives in saltflats.

☛ The lizard's tail has heart-shaped leaves and a tail-like spike that inspired this perennial herb's name.

☛ When in full bloom, the heart-shaped leaves of the pickerel-weed wrap themselves around blue, tubular flowers.

☛ Creamy white flowers with a brush of crimson in their centers identify the rose or marsh mallow, a tall, hairy-stemmed perennial herb that thrives in the Piedmont and the Coastal Plain.

☛ The seashore mallow has a similar flower to the rose or marsh mallow, but it's smaller and pink.

☛ The sparsely leaved, square-stemmed tearthumb thrives in wet fields and marshlands throughout the state.

☛ The water-horehound, or bugleweed, is an interesting member of the mint family, with clusters of white flowers growing around the base of each leaf.

Beautiful But Deadly
North Carolina has hundreds of poisonous plants. Here are a few that you might want to avoid when you're exploring the state's wild areas:

☛ The calla lily, or florist's calla, is a bridal favorite, but don't do anything more than smell this beauty. All parts of the calla lily are poisonous, and eating it could be fatal.

☛ With names such as apricot, apple-of-Peru, asparagus fern and black cherry, one would think these plants must be safe to eat. After all, they're named after edible fruits and vegetables. But names, like appearances, can be deceiving. The leaves and twigs of the apricot plant can cause anything from general weakness to coma, and exactly which parts of the apple-of-Peru, or shoofly plant, are poisonous is still questionable, but it is listed as a poisonous plant because it is closely related to well-known toxic plants. The berries of the asparagus fern can irritate your skin and cause gastrointestinal problems, and the leaves, twigs and seeds of the black or wild cherry cause gasping, spasms and respiratory failure, among other difficulties.

BY THE NUMBERS

Counting Heads

According to 2008 estimates from the U.S. Census Bureau, North Carolina had a population of about 9,222,313, making it the 11th most populated state in the U.S. In 2000, there were 3,132,013 households in the state, with an average of 2.49 persons living in each household.

The Municipal Picture
There are at least 100 municipalities in North Carolina with populations larger than 5000. Here are the top 10, according to 2006 estimates from the State Data Center:

Rank	Municipality	County	Population
1	Charlotte	Mecklenburg	651,562
2	Raleigh	Wake	352,919
3	Greensboro	Guilford	241,753

5	Winston-Salem	Forsyth	201,955
6	Fayetteville	Cumberland	173,898
7	Cary	Wake	122,139
8	Wilmington	New Hanover	98,529
9	High Point	Guilford	95,630
10	Asheville	Buncombe	75,948

DID YOU KNOW?

Charlotte is the 18th largest city in the U.S.

The Big Three
The state's three main cities are Charlotte, Raleigh and Wilmington.

North Carolina NUGGET The City of Raleigh made history in July 2006. That's when its population hit the 350,000-person mark and kept on going!

The "Have Nots"

Based on 2007 figures, an estimated 14.3 percent of the state's population lives below the poverty line.

Averaging It Out
North Carolina has an average of 165.2 people per square mile, based on a Census 2000 population estimate of 8,046,406.

Find Your Center

The unincorporated community of Erect is considered North Carolina's "center of population," which is officially defined as the "geographical point that describes a center point of the region's population."

Evenly Split?

There's a fairly even distribution of males and females in North Carolina, but the females have a slight lead, representing 51 percent of the population.

Coming of Age

The median age of North Carolina residents is 35.8 years. About 7.1 percent of the population is under five years of age, 24.3 percent is under 18 years old, and 12.4 percent of the population is aged 65 years and older.

DID YOU KNOW?

There are about 1,540,365 people aged five and older who are living with a disability.

Make Room for More

According to Census 2000 figures and 2008 estimates, North Carolina has experienced a 14.6 percent population increase, which is higher than the country's overall eight percent population increase

High Marks?

About 78.1 percent of the population aged 25 and older have earned a high school diploma, which is slightly less than the national average of 80.4 percent. Regarding post-secondary education, 22.5 percent of the population aged 25 and older has a bachelor's degree or higher, which is also lower than the national average of 24.4 percent.

Legal Aliens

About 5.3 percent of North Carolina's population reported they were "foreign born" on their 2000 census forms.

Bringing Home the Bacon
The median household income in North Carolina, based on 2007 figures, was $44,772.

Making the Commute

According to Census 2000 figures, it took people 24.0 minutes to travel to and from their place of employment.

North Carolina's Population Through the Years
North Carolina's first official population figures were published in 1790, and the state was already well populated, with 393,751 residents. By 1850, the population had grown considerably, to 869,039 residents. Here's the breakdown since then:

Census Year	Population
1860	992,622
1880	1,399,750
1900	1,893,810
1950	4,061,929
2000	8,046,406
2008	9,222,313

Largest Leap

The biggest 10-year population jump occurred between the years 1870, when the state registered a population of 1,071,361, and 1880, when new figures revealed 1,399,750 residents. That change represented a 30.7 percent population increase.

Break It Down
According to 2008 census estimates:

☛ 73.9 percent of the population is white, including 7.4 percent that is of Hispanic or Latino origin

☛ 21.6 percent of the population is African American

☛ 1.3 percent of the population is American Indian and Alaskan Native

☛ 1.9 percent of the population is Asian

☛ 0.1 percent of the population is Native Hawaiian and other Pacific Islander

Religious Diversity

About 84 percent of North Carolina's population call themselves Christians, and about 41 percent of these Christians say they're Evangelical Protestant. Another 21 percent call themselves Mainline Protestant, 13 percent are Black Protestant, and nine percent are Roman Catholic. About one percent of the population follows the Buddhist faith, another three percent list themselves as participants of "other religions," and 12 percent say they are non-religious.

Baby, Oh Baby!

In 2007, the State Center for Health Statistics reported the following as the top 10 picks for baby names for boys and girls born in North Carolina:

Boys	Girls
William	Madison
Jacob	Emma
Christopher	Emily
Joshua	Ava
Ethan	Abigail
Michael	Olivia
James	Hannah
Noah	Elizabeth
Daniel	Addison
Elijah	Isabella

First Inhabitants

Native Americans were the first humans to inhabit this great country we call home, living on the land and taming the landscape. What follows is a breakdown of some of those traditional tribes, thanks to information gathered by Access Genealogy:

☛ The Cape Fear Indians lived near Cape Fear. Their specific Native designation isn't clear, as is much of their history and language.

☛ The Catawba peoples lived near the Catawba River, in the southwestern part of the state.

☛ It's believed the Cheraw Indians originally lived in the Pickens and Oconee counties of South Carolina, but they eventually migrated north and settled in the area of Henderson, Polk and Rutherford counties.

☛ The mountains in the western portion of North Carolina were traditionally home to the Cherokee.

☛ The Chowanoc, on the other hand, were river people, living on the Chowan River, near the junction of the Meherrin and Blackwater rivers.

☛ The Coree or Coranine lived in Craven and Carteret counties.

☛ The Eno River, located in what's known today as Orange and Durham counties, was traditionally home to the Eno tribe.

☛ The Hatteras traditionally inhabited Cape Hatteras and Roanoke Island.

☛ The Keyauwee settled on the boundary between North and South Carolina. Over time, the Keyauwee either died out or were assimilated into the Catawba.

☛ The Lumbee are still prevalent in the Robeson County town of Pembroke.

☛ The Machapunga, a people with Algonquian affiliations, primarily lived in Hyde County, but there is some evidence that smaller populations of Machapunga also lived in Dare, Tyrrell, Washington and parts of Beaufort counties.

☛ The North Carolina representation of the Meherrin tribe lived in what's now known as Hertford County.

☛ The Hiwassee River area was home to the Natchez people before their tribe fractured and most members attached themselves to the Cherokee.

☞ The Occaneechi lived along the banks of Virginia's Roanoke River, but there is evidence that they traveled through what are now the North Carolina counties of Warren, Halifax and Northampton.

☞ The Pamlico once lived along the Pamlico River before they were almost completely eradicated by smallpox in 1696. The Tuscarora were believed to have taken any survivors as slaves.

☞ The Saponi lived along one of North Carolina's longest rivers, the Yadkin. There is some evidence of the Saponi living in Virginia as well.

☞ The Shakori people were so nomadic that there's not much known about their traditional lands. It is thought that they mingled with the Eno and therefore quite likely lived in today's counties of Franklin, Vance and Warren.

☞ The southern portion of Alamance County was home to the Sissipahaw.

☞ Mecklenburg County was home to the Sugeree.

☞ The Tuscarora peoples lived along the shores of the Tar, Pamlico, Roanoke and Neuse rivers.

☞ Bertie County was once home to the Tutelo.

☞ It is believed that the Waccamaw followed the Waccamaw River north from South Carolina to settle in North Carolina.

☞ The upper portion of the Yadkin River was once home to the Wateree.

☞ The Waxhaw migrated to North Carolina from South Carolina. On arrival, they settled in what's now known as Union County.

☛ The Weapemeoc tribe was supposedly named after a particular place, but there's no proof to back the claim. The tribe was also known as the Yeopim.

☛ It's believed that the Woccon lived in the area of present day Goldsboro and Wayne counties.

DID YOU  KNOW?

The only federally recognized tribe remaining in the state is the Eastern Band of Cherokee Indians of North Carolina.

Growth Spurt

According to Census 2000, the population of North Carolina grew by 21.4 percent between 1990 and 2000, making it one of the fastest growing states in the country. Only eight other states showed a higher percentage increase: Arizona, Colorado, Florida, Georgia, Idaho, Nevada, Texas and Utah.

ROADSIDE ATTRACTIONS

The Old Burying Ground

Walking through a graveyard can provide visitors with an understanding of the history of an area and a feel for the kind of people who once lived there. This is definitely the case with the Old Burying Ground. Located near the town of Beaufort and officially deeded to that community in 1731, many of the grave markers in this cemetery are so old that it's nearly impossible to read them. According to one tourism website, the oldest legible marker is dated 1756. Still, Civil War stories, local legends and history about the people buried there have been collected, as much as possible, and preserved for residents and visitors alike. Here are some interesting bits of information on the Old Burying Ground:

☞ It is one of the oldest cemeteries in North Carolina.

☞ The graveyard was listed in the magazine *Our State* and the book *100 Most Romantic Places in North Carolina* as a must-see destination.

☞ More than 400 folks are buried here.

☞ Many of the graves face east, ensuring that the people buried there would "be facing the sun when they arose on judgment morn."

☞ One little girl who'd been traveling with her father, a merchant captain, died on the return voyage from England. Bound by a promise he'd made to the child's mother to return with the little girl, the father preserved her body in a keg of rum. She is buried in this graveyard, and legend has it that children in the area have decorated her grave for more than 250 years. The day after toys or gifts are laid on the grave, they go missing, and the story is that the girl's ghost moves them or plays with them.

☞ A privateer named Otway Burns is buried here, alongside the cannon from his ship.

☞ During the Revolutionary War, a dying soldier who had been shot in the area begged his comrades to bury him in an upright position, in full uniform and facing England in a full salute to King George.

Britain's Little Corner

On Ocracoke Island, the bodies of four British soldiers washed up on shore around May 14, 1942. Their ship, the HMS *Bedfordshire*, was torpedoed and sunk by a German U-boat. The bodies of the men were carried to a small cemetery and buried honorably, with four grave markers. A lease for the 2290-square-foot plot of land, known as the British Cemetery, was given to the Commonwealth War Graves

Committee and will officially remain British soil as long as it continues to be a graveyard.

DID YOU  KNOW?

A plaque in the British Cemetery sums up the reasons why Ocracoke residents made sure the four British soldiers received a proper burial. The words on the plaque, written by Robert Brooke, relay the following sentiment:

> *If I should die think only this of me that there's some forever corner of a foreign field that is forever England.*

Fine Arts
The Mattie King Davis Art Gallery is a favorite stop for art lovers looking to appreciate a variety of mediums and expressions. Along with the traditional oil and watercolor paintings, the gallery also exhibits jewelry, pottery, photography and more. The gallery is located in Beaufort's historic Rustell House, which was built in 1732.

Thrill-Seeker's Haven

A barren patch of land near Bennett, an unincorporated community located on the border of Chatham and Randolph counties, has attracted both scientists and inquisitive folks with a taste for the macabre. It's all because of a 40-foot, circular patch of ground in the midst of the forest that local folks say nothing, not even the most durable weed, has grown on for at least 100 years. Scientists from the U.S. Geological Survey have examined the land and can provide no explanation for the phenomenon. Local legends, however, provide a reason for the site's barrenness. John William Harden (1903–85), a journalist from Greensboro, reported that Chatham residents called the place the "Devil's Tramping Ground." In a 1949 article, Harden wrote that the legend suggests the Devil visits the site nightly, pacing in circles while thinking up new ways to curse humankind. "There, sometimes during the dark of night, the Majesty of the Underworld of Evil silently tramps around that bare circle—thinking, plotting and planning against good and in behalf of wrong….So far as is known, no person has ever spent the night there to disprove this is what happens." To this day, it's believed that no one has successfully endured an entire night at the site.

Decorative Gourds

Marvin and Mary Johnson of Angier initially began what developed into the Gourd Museum in order to help one of their children with a project. By 1965, the family was overwhelmed with gourds made into everything from useful vessels to decorative items, and being the lovely husband that he was, Marvin moved the gourds into a "house" of their own. For the next several decades, the couple grew more than 200 varieties of gourds, and they arranged, painted and decorated these ornamental veggies, winning all kinds of ribbons from local fairs for their efforts. Mary and then Marvin passed away and their farm was sold. Today, you can visit the Marvin and Mary Johnson Gourd Museum at the Angier Municipal Building.

One-of-a-Kind Collection
The Belhaven Memorial Museum in Belhaven houses a wide assortment of memorabilia significant to local history. But perhaps its most unique collection of local "artifacts" is the more than 30,000 items acquired following the death of Mrs. Eva Blount Way. Born in 1869, Eva moved to Beech Ridge just outside Belhaven when she married at the age of 17. She lived her entire 76 years after her marriage at that location, and during that time, she amassed a huge assortment of personal items (such as Christmas treasures), as well as a huge collection of other people's things that she just couldn't bring herself to discard (such as the 225 hosiery boxes and a 10-inch-wide ball of string).

Heavenly Hammock

The Hatteras Hammock Company of San Diego, California, is responsible for what they'd like to believe is a world record. The company was commissioned to make a 40-foot-long, 12-foot-wide hammock for a young North Carolina State University fellow pledging his fraternity. The latest account of the roadside attraction was that the hammock was perched beside the Nags Head Hammock store in Point Harbor. It was apparently constructed out of 10,000 feet of rope and can hold up to 8000 pounds.

Ho-Ho-Ho!

Tucked away in Cherokee is a little hideaway that is apparently visited quite regularly by the jolly, white-bearded Santa we all know and love. Santa's Village and Zoo Land is open from May to November, giving youngsters a chance to chat with Santa and get in their special requests well in advance of the Christmas rush. Visitors can watch a magic show at the Jingle Bell Theater, lunch at the snack bar, receive a "Good Conduct Diploma"—to be kept at all costs to ensure that Santa remembers they've made it onto the "nice list"—and shop at Frosty's T-Shirt Shop. If you're just hurtin' for Christmas in July, this is definitely the place to go.

North Carolina NUGGET The Occoneechee Speedway, opened in 1949, was one of two NASCAR tracks to open that year. It's also the only original track still in use, and the Occoneechee Speedway is named on the National Register of Historic Places.

Elaborate Pastime

Henry L. Warren was fixated on an ongoing project on his property near Yanceyville (Prospect Hill). Named Shangri-la, it is a miniature village small enough to house all the leprechauns in North Carolina. From 1968 until he died in 1978, Warren, with the help of his neighbor Junius Pennix, built 28 miniature stone houses, complete with red-and-white trim and all the ornamentation you can imagine. Visitors to the Hillsborough area can acquire directions from the tourist bureau.

Have a Seat!
Thomasville is home to the world's largest Duncan Phyfe chair. So, what exactly *is* a Duncan Phyfe chair? Well, Phyfe was a Scottish furniture maker known for his simple style. In 1922, the Thomasville Chair Company erected a huge homage to the Scot—an 18-foot-high, steel-and-concrete armchair right in the middle of the downtown. Imagine the size of the matching footrest! The town even got President Lyndon B. Johnson to travel there to sit in the chair.

Bureau of Information
Put a sock in it! How about a pair of them? The world's largest chest of drawers was built in 1926 by the High Point Chamber of Commerce. The original structure was roughly 20 feet tall and was the office for the Chamber. In 1996, the chest was completely renovated into a 38-foot-tall monstrosity—in the mold of a Goddard-Townsend block-front chest.

The High Point Jaycees now use the monument for their base of operations. Two socks currently hang out of the middle drawer and, yes, they are clean.

DID YOU KNOW?

Aside from the freestanding 38-foot-tall chest of drawers in High Point, there's another large piece of furniture in town that is almost three times as tall. At Furnitureland South, you can find an 80-foot-tall chest of drawers attached to the side of the building. Imagine the size of the clothes that go in it!

Thou Shalt Not Miss These

Moses would definitely be impressed. Located in Murphy, near the Great Smoky Mountains, wayward travelers can journey through Fields of the Wood Bible Park. One of the park's main attractions is Ten Commandments Mountain, which the world's largest New Testament calls home. The 300-foot-high scripture's letters and numerals are four feet wide by five feet high and can even be seen from outer space! You can hike up to the top of the mountain and read the Commandments from a peaceful overlook.

MUST-SEE NC

More Than Just a Road
Started on September 11, 1935, as a Depression-era public-works project, the picturesque Blue Ridge Parkway has become "America's favorite drive." The nation's first (and longest— 469 miles) rural parkway connects Shenandoah National Park to the north and Great Smoky Mountains National Park to the south. In the fall, when the leaves on the mountain trees are a-changin', there is no prettier view in the world.

Check Out These Numbers

Biodiversity is very important to National Park Service workers along the Blue Ridge Parkway. The following evidence of life can be found along "America's favorite drive":

- 600 streams (150 headwaters)

- 47 Natural Heritage Areas (areas set aside as national, regional or state examples of exemplary natural communities)

- About 100 different soil types

- 75 distinct plant communities (including 24 considered globally rare, and seven of these considered globally imperiled)

- 14 major vegetation types

- About 1600 vascular plant species (the second highest number of vascular plants for any national park; 50 are threatened or endangered)

- Nearly 100 species of trees (about as many as are found in all of Europe)

- Almost 400 species of mosses

- Nearly 2000 species of fungi

☛ 54 different mammal species

☛ More than 40 species of both salamanders and reptiles

☛ 159 species of birds

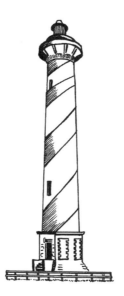

Light Up the Darkness

With the "Graveyard of the Atlantic" threatening ships' captains sailing through the North Carolina waterways, lighthouses have been a necessary and welcome sight since the turn of the 19th century. Tourists from all over the world come to the Outer Banks and surrounding areas to see these brick-and-mortar guardians of the coast.

☛ **Currituck Beach Lighthouse (Active)**
   Built: 1875 (Corolla)
   Height: 162 feet
   Steps: 214
   Tidbit: The last brick lighthouse built on the Outer Banks

☛ **Bodie "Body" Island Lighthouse (Active)**
Built: 1872 (third version, four miles north of Oregon Inlet)
Height: 156 feet
Steps: 214
Tidbit: Each exterior stripe is 22 feet high

☛ **Cape Hatteras Lighthouse (Active)**
Built: 1870 (Hatteras Island—the first tower was built in 1802)
Height: 198 feet
Steps: 257
Tidbit: The world's tallest brick lighthouse and the only
   lighthouse to be moved because of erosion concerns

☛ **Ocracoke Island Lighthouse (Active)**
Built: 1823 (Ocracoke)
Height: 75 feet
Steps: 220 (climbing not allowed)
Tidbit: The oldest NC lighthouse still in continuous service
   and the second oldest in the U.S.

☛ **Cape Lookout Lighthouse (Active)**
Built: 1859 (Cape Lookout)
Height: 163 feet
Steps: 269
Tidbit: The first "tall" lighthouse built on the Outer Banks

☛ **Bald Head Island Lighthouse, also known as "Old Baldy"**
(Inactive; decommissioned in 1935)
Built: 1818 (Bald Head Island)
Height: 110 feet
Steps: 108
Tidbit: The oldest standing lighthouse in North Carolina

☛ **Oak Island Lighthouse (Active)**
Built: 1958 (Oak Island)
Height: 169 feet
Steps: 134 ("ladder" style)
Tidbit: One of the newest lighthouses in the U.S.

☛ **Price's Creek Light (Inactive; partially in ruins)**
Built: 1848 (Cape Fear River)
Height: 20 feet
Steps: n/a
Tidbit: It was used as a Confederate signal station during the
Civil War

☛ **Roanoke River Light (Inactive; decommissioned in 1941)**
Built: 1867 (Plymouth, since moved to Edenton)
Height: Two-story building
Steps: n/a
Tidbit: The last remaining screw-pile lighthouse in the U.S.

DID YOU  KNOW?

The diamond shapes that decorate the Cape Lookout Lighthouse
were not just to point out the Diamond Shoals or to distinguish
it from Cape Hatteras' famous diagonal stripes or Bodie Island's
horizontals. The side tips of the diamonds point north and south
through the treacherous waterway that has felled many a ship.

A Mile High

The swinging bridge at Grandfather Mountain might be a challenge for anyone with a touch of vertigo. The 228-foot-long
Mile High Swinging Bridge stretches across an 80-foot gap at
Grandfather Mountain's Linville Peak. It was built in 1952
at a cost of $15,000 and dedicated by North Carolina governor
William B. Umstead. In 1999, it was clear that the giant
structure, which actually swings freely one mile above the valley below, needed to be rebuilt. The cost of this refurbishing
was in the neighborhood of $300,000.

Deep in the Heart of Humpback Mountain
In 1822, a man on a fishing expedition in the Blue Ridge
Mountains saw fish swimming in and out of what seemed to
be solid rock. Figuring that there had to be something to this,

Henry R. Colton decided to "dig" a little deeper (pardon the pun) into the phenomenon. Colton and this group of fishermen were the first white men to "discover" the formations that probably began taking shape over 30 million years ago.

Linville Caverns, North Carolina's only "show" caverns, opened for tours in 1939 and allowed people to experience the underground environment of the world's oldest mountain range. Visitors can enjoy Bottomless Lake, an estimated 250-foot-deep lighted body of water deep inside the caverns. During the winter and early spring months, visitors can also see the hibernating eastern pipistrelle bat hanging along the ceiling inside the caves. Be careful not to disturb them, as that might be fatal to the bats. Local legend says that Civil War deserters used the caves to hide from their military units, as evidence of rudimentary campfires was found in the central caverns. Legend also says that smoke from those campfires betrayed the deserters when it became visible outside the hiding spot. Where there's smoke, right?

DID YOU  **KNOW?**

You'll need to bring a jacket to Linville Caverns. The temperature is a cool 52°F year round.

Fontana Dam
The 480-foot-high Fontana Dam was completed in 1944 and stretches 2365 feet across the Little Tennessee River. It is the highest dam east of the Rocky Mountains and the uppermost of five dams on the Little Tennessee River. The famous Appalachian Trail, which stretches over 2000 miles from Georgia to Maine, crosses over the Fontana Dam. Hot showers are located at the dam's trail shelter, and hikers have dubbed them the Fontana Hilton.

Native North Carolinians

Most people do not realize that the state encompasses another country. The quiet mountainside town of Cherokee is home to the Eastern Band of the Cherokee Indians. The tribe's lands lie mainly in Swain County near the Great Smoky Mountains and in Jackson County. Most of the original peoples in this area were not forced to take part in the Trail of Tears, the tragic march of the Cherokee westward to Oklahoma. They hid in the hills and surrounding mountains and fought furiously to stay in their homeland. Because of that refusal, the Eastern Band is not affiliated with the Cherokee Nation or the United Keetoowah Band of Cherokee Indians, except on a historical or cultural level.

Once in the Qualla Boundary, as the reservation is known, visitors can experience a real, working Cherokee settlement from around 1759 at the Oconaluftee Indian Village. Want to see a canoe hulled? Want to see traditional Cherokee medicine practiced? Want to see some awesome beadwork or pottery? Then Oconaluftee is the place to be. There's also Qualla Arts & Crafts, the oldest and leading Native American Arts cooperative in the United States, founded in 1946.

DID YOU KNOW?

Scott Stapp, lead singer of the band Creed, was born in Cherokee on August 8, 1973.

Woulda, Coulda, Shoulda…

Cherokee Chief Junaluska was born in the NC mountains around 1776 and saved General (soon to be President) Andrew Jackson's life at the Battle of Horseshoe Bend in the War of 1812. When the removal of the Cherokee began in 1838, Junaluska reportedly said, "If I had known that Jackson would drive us from our homes, I would have killed him that day at the Horseshoe."

Unto These Hills

The nation's second-longest-running (and third-oldest) outdoor drama, *Unto These Hills*, depicts the story of the faithful Cherokee who fought to save their land. Written by Kermit Hunter, the outdoor drama opened on July 1, 1950, in a mountainside theater that was designed by the architect of the Manteo Waterside Theatre—home of *The Lost Colony*.

DID YOU KNOW?

Academy Award–winning actor Morgan Freeman and *Smallville's* Michael Rosenbaum (Lex Luthor) have acted in *Unto These Hills*.

Jockey's Ridge

Jockey's Ridge, the tallest natural sand dune on the East Coast, is one of the most significant landmarks on the Outer Banks. Over one million people visit the 420-acre natural state park every year. Three distinct environments are present in the park: the dunes, maritime thickets and the Roanoke Sound estuary. There's lots of wind and soft sand here, which is why the Wright Brothers chose this area to test their *Wright Flyer*. If anyone ever tells you to "Go fly a kite," then come to Jockey's Ridge—you won't be alone.

North Carolina NUGGET If you're venturing out to see Jockey's Ridge in the summer, bring some shoes. The sand on the dunes is incredibly hot during the summer months. On average, the sand is 25°F to 30°F degrees hotter than the air temperature, so when it's 95°F, the sand will be 125°F. Yikes!

GHOST STORIES AND FOLK LEGENDS

First in Fright

Taking part in every major battle in the Pacific during World War II, the battleship *North Carolina* was decommissioned in June 1947. The ship made its final voyage in 1960, docking in Wilmington as a National Landmark. Once you're aboard the war monument, that's when the fun starts.

Crew members have experienced hatches opening and closing at random, lights and TVs turning on and off, not to mention unexpectedly cold blasts of air on hot North Carolina summer days. Ghost hunters from Haunted North Carolina Paranormal Research & Investigations went on board and found that all three of their camera batteries (fully charged and scattered in different places across the ship) died at the *exact* same time— 9:35 PM. Ironically, this was about three minutes after one of the researchers spotted what he thought was movement in the Chaplain's Office.

Sometimes months, even years, go by with no occurence of the weird phenomena. But if you're in the Wilmington area, take a chance. Literally.

Don't Lose Your Head

There is legend in the sleepy little Wayne County town of Fremont that people from all over the state have tried to verify. As the story goes, a local man was a little tipsy one night and decided to walk along the railroad tracks through town. Somehow, he was struck by a train and lost his head. It has been reported that, on cold and foggy nights, a light can be seen floating up and down along the tracks. Locals say it is the man trying to find his missing head. Some stories have been told—probably to scare ghost hunters—that say if the "man" catches up to you, you may die. Others have said that if the light is coming toward you and you run to your car, the car will not start. There's only one way to find out.

Leave No Stone Unturned

If you're familiar with Shakespeare's *Romeo and Juliet*, then the Chapel Hill legend of Peter Dromgoole and Fannie will be easy to understand. In 1833, 18-year-old Dromgoole and another University of North Carolina (UNC) student were both in love with a local girl named Fanny. As the story goes, the two men argued and then challenged each other to a duel. As you can imagine, dueling was discouraged in the UNC student handbook. When the shots rang out on top of Piney Prospect, Dromgoole took a bullet to the heart. He collapsed against a huge rock, his blood pouring out onto the porous stone. The other man and his second furiously dug a shallow grave into which they put the body, then rolled the enormous rock over it in an attempt to hide their bloody deed.

Unaware that her beloved was dead, Fanny came to Piney Prospect time and time again, waiting for Peter to appear. The ironic thing, according to legend, is that Peter and Fanny had fallen in love and talked about their future at the very site of his death—where she lost him forever.

According to one version of the legend, at the rock where Peter died, Fanny would occasionally see him walking toward her, but he would disappear before reaching her. She would then lean against the rock and sob silently, unaware that her lover was buried underneath her feet. Like in a fairy tale, Fanny died a short time later, presumably from a broken heart. Rumor has it that Peter and Fanny's ghosts still haunt Gimghoul Castle, conveniently built in 1924 near Piney Prospect and the site of their unending love. The stone can be found near the castle and is marked with strange brown discolorations. It's called—you guessed it—Dromgoole's Rock.

DID YOU KNOW?

Gimghoul Castle is located on the UNC campus in Chapel Hill. It is the home of the Order of Gimghoul, a secret collegiate society similar to Yale's Skull and Bones Society. Formed in 1889, the society was originally called the Order of the Dromgoole.

The Great White Hope

The Diamond Shoals off the North Carolina coast have long been treacherous waterways for sea captains passing through. However, coastal legend speaks of an unexpected helper that once aided those captains through the dangerous Hatteras Inlet. An albino dolphin, which first appeared around 1790, would guide sailors through the shifting sandbars and strong currents. Nicknamed "Hatteras Jack," the dolphin became trusted by seafarers, who navigated through the inlet with its help. Captains would seek out Jack, blowing their foghorns when they got close to the dangerous waters. The government eventually stepped in and marked the channel, and Hatteras Jack began appearing less and less frequently. Finally, the dolphin disappeared altogether, apparently knowing its work was done.

DID YOU KNOW?

Seven kinds of dolphins are found off the North Carolina coast:

- ☛ saddleback dolphin (*Delphinus delphis*)—rare

- ☛ grampus or Risso's dolphin (*Grampus griseus*)—rare

- ☛ striped dolphin (*Stenella coeruleoalba*)—rare

- ☛ spinner dolphin (*Stenella longirostris*)—rare

- ☛ Atlantic spotted dolphin (*Stenella frontalis*)—rare

- ☛ rough-toothed dolphin (*Steno bredanensis*)—rare

- ☛ Atlantic bottlenose dolphin (*Tursiops truncates*)—common

North Carolina NUGGET If you're going to be sailing through North Carolina's Diamond Shoals, make sure to have a six-toed cat with you. Legend says that such a cat is good luck.

She's a Witch! Burn Her! Wait, Where'd She Go?

Very few people have heard the story of the strange woman who lived alone in the small Brigands' Bay community of Frisco, but evidence of her exists to this day. According to coastal legend, a woman by the name of Cora lived in the tiny town in the early 1700s. The only company she kept was a baby she carried everywhere. People became suspicious of Cora when a cow went dry and stopped giving milk after she touched it, a boy who mocked her baby became very sick and almost died, and although fishermen were unable to catch fish, Cora always seemed to have a fresh supply.

One day, Captain Eli Blood and his ship, the *Susan G*, foundered in waters near Brigands' Bay, and he took up residence in the town to await word from the ship's owner. Blood was a longtime resident of Salem, Massachusetts, and was determined to find out if Cora was a witch after hearing all the local stories about her. He tried to cut her hair but could not because it "was tougher than wire rope." Then Blood threw her into the sound, where she floated face down. From his Salem experience, Blood decided that both incidents were definite signs that Cora was indeed a witch.

Convinced of her guilt, Captain Blood tied Cora and her baby to a huge oak tree in the center of town, determined to burn the witch. Kindling was placed at her feet, and a rope was secured tightly around them. Before Blood could light the fire, a huge storm cloud formed overhead. Then a tremendous bolt of lightning struck the tree, creating a massive amount of smoke. When the smoke cleared, the kindling was untouched and the rope was still in place, but Cora and the baby were gone. However, the letters "CORA" were deeply burned into the bark of the oak tree.

DID YOU  **KNOW?**

The Cora Tree still stands at Brigands' Bay, resting comfortably on Snug Harbor Drive. Go see CORA for yourself—the letters are still quite visible, even though the tree is over 300 years old.

Is It Chilly in Here, or Is It Just Me?

On January 11, 1886, the Philadelphia-based schooner *Crissie Wright* was on her way from Baltimore to Savannah. It was one of the coldest months locals had ever seen, and some say it has never been as cold since. On this particular day, a horrible storm came up and caught the *Crissie Wright* at sea. The ship's main mast brace parted under the strain of the weather, causing the ship to run aground near Shackleford Banks. Wave after wave crashed over the *Crissie Wright*, and locals could not launch their rescue boats because the blizzard was too severe. People on shore could only watch as the crewmen lashed themselves to the rigging. Bonfires were built in the hope that the men could make it to shore, but the breakers were much too fierce. The night became bitterly cold, cold in an eerie sort of way. Residents watched in utter horror as the waves swept several of the sailors overboard, never to be seen again.

The next morning, residents found three men frozen to death in the rigging and the ship's cook barely alive. The three men were buried in Beaufort's Old Burying Ground under a common grave marker, and some still refer to this tragedy today. On a really cold day, you might hear a Beaufort resident say, "Whew, it's as cold tonight as the night the *Crissie Wright* came ashore." This story is a chiller of major proportions.

THE LOST COLONY

The Nation's First Mystery

I don't know about you, but I love a good mystery. You know all the players, but you have *no* clue whodunit. Well, North Carolina is home to America's first and best-known mystery—that of the "Lost Colony" of Roanoke. Sir Walter Raleigh sent two men—Philip Amadas and Arthur Barlowe—to the New World in 1584 to scout locations for a new British colony. Raleigh later sponsored Ralph Lane and a group of English settlers to "colonize" and "dominate" the area around Roanoke Island. Lane's tactics with the Croatan Indians were antagonistic and belligerent, and he often kidnapped and killed the Croatans for supplies and information. Lane's colony soon ran low on supplies, and the colonists hitched a ride back to England with famed privateer Sir Francis Drake.

A short time later, Raleigh tried again, sending John White and a total of 117 colonists back to the original colony. Against his better judgment, White resettled the Roanoke colony, even though he had wanted to move north toward Chesapeake Bay. Again, the colony ran low on supplies, and the colonists suggested that White go back to England to replenish the necessary items, which he agreed to do. By this time, White's daughter, Eleanor Dare, had given birth to the first English child born on the soil of the New World, Virginia Dare.

White set sail for England, but he was obstructed by the Spanish Armada and the waters off the coast of England were a war zone, so his return to the colony was delayed by several months. When he arrived back at Roanoke in 1590, he found the area deserted. No sign of life, no sign of anything except for two things—the word "Croatoan" was carved into one tree, and "Cro" was carved into a second tree.

Where did the colonists go? Where was his granddaughter Virginia? No one truly knows for sure what happened. Some say that when the colonists had depleted their supplies, they headed north toward the Chesapeake area, only to be caught in the middle of two warring Native American tribes and killed. Another story says that the colonists were absorbed into the native Croatan tribe, mixing English and Indian bloodlines. The modern Lumbee Indians in the state might very well be their descendants.

Without actual proof, or a very *very* old eyewitness, we will likely never really know what happened to the "Lost Colony" and Virginia Dare.

DID YOU KNOW?

Sir Walter Raleigh grew up in the house of a farmer, Hayes Barton, near Devon, England. Hayes Barton is a name that has carried over to North Carolina's capital city, with a beautiful neighborhood named after him near Five Points (listed on the National Register of Historic Places), a couple of churches (Hayes Barton Baptist and Hayes Barton United Methodist), a bakery (Hayes Barton Café and Dessertry), a veterinary hospital (Hayes Barton Animal Hospital) and so on and so forth.

The White Doe

Of the many legends of the whereabouts of Virginia Dare, the tale of the ghostly White Doe of Roanoke is one of the most famous. In 1901, Sallie Southall Cotton penned a long narrative entitled *The White Doe: The Fate of Virginia Dare (an Indian legend)*. In this narrative, Cotton tells of young Virginia Dare, who was raised by the friendly Manteo people. She became a beautiful young woman, desired by two tribesmen, and her Indian name was Winona-Ska. One chieftain, Okisko, was convinced that he would marry Winona-Ska. Another tribesman, an old witch doctor named Chico, wanted Winona-Ska all to himself. When Winona-Ska rebuffed the witch doctor's advances, he turned her into a majestic, snow-white doe, thinking that if he couldn't have her, no man ever would. Okisko desperately wanted to break the spell, so he found a magician who gave him a special arrow. The arrow, when dipped into a magic fountain, turned into pearl. If Okisko's pearl arrow pierced the doe's heart, Chico's spell would be broken.

However, there was another plan afoot. Wanchese, the son of the Indian who John Smith took back to England (also named Wanchese), wanted the doe dead. His father had been given a silver arrow by Queen Elizabeth I, and silver was the only thing that could kill the doe.

Okisko spotted the white doe one afternoon and took advantage of the opportunity. He sighted on the doe's heart and let fly his magical arrow. But just as his pearl arrow pierced the doe's heart, so did Wanchese's silver arrow. The spell was broken, but Winona-Ska died in Okisko's arms.

Okisko took both arrows back to the magic fountain and prayed for Winona-Ska's life to be restored. When he returned to the place where she had died, there was no sign of either the doe or the young woman. A short time later, the doe appeared to Okisko again, looked deeply into his eyes and disappeared back into the woods. Some residents of the Roanoke Island area still claim to have spotted a ghostly white doe. Is it Winona-Ska, waiting for her pearl arrow? Seeing as how this story has existed almost as long as the state has, it kinda makes you wonder.

The Play's the Thing...

America's first and longest-running symphonic outdoor drama started right here in the Tar Heel State. Debuting in 1937, *The Lost Colony* tells of Sir Walter Raleigh's failed Roanoke colony and of the life and mystery of Virginia Dare. Millions of people have seen this historical play, which focus on the 117 English men, women and children whose fate became the nation's first mystery. The play is performed in the Wayside Theatre at Fort Raleigh in Manteo—the site of the original Roanoke colony.

 *Lost Colony* playwright Paul Green won the Pulitzer Prize in 1927 for his first play, *In Abraham's Bosom*. He is also a graduate of my alma mater, Campbell University in Buies Creek.

DID YOU KNOW?

There were some television commercials back in the day in which NC's favorite TV sheriff, Andy Griffith, invited young and old alike down to Manteo to see *The Lost Colony*. Griffith actually starred in the symphonic outdoor drama as Sir Walter Raleigh.

History on a Stick

In 1935, the state legislature established the North Carolina Highway Historical Marker Program. Etched in iron and visible from the highway, these little bits of "history on a stick" span the gamut from presidential birthplaces to famous duels between Carolinians. NC's program is one of the oldest such programs in continuous operation in the nation. Why am I suddenly seeing visions of comedian Jeff Dunham and a talking jalapeño in my head?

FOUNDING FATHERS AND FLYERS

Who Gets the Credit?

With North Carolina being one of the first original sites of English colonization, there could be several people up for the title of "North Carolina's Founding Father/Mother/Person." An argument could be made for King Charles II, since he granted the charter for the creation of the territory first called "Carolina" in 1663. Some would say the 83 delegates who signed the Halifax Resolves could be contenders for the title, since that document was the first action toward American independence from England. Others might say that William Hooper, Joseph Hewes and John Penn are the top contenders, since they were the delegates from North Carolina who signed the Declaration of Independence in 1776. Richard Caswell was the first governor of North Carolina under the new state Constitution (they rejected the U.S. Constitution and created their own), so maybe he should be considered a candidate. This is beginning to sound like a "Who came first, the chicken or the egg" argument. Either way, credit for creating this great state lies in many hands.

No, *We're* First in Flight!

It's a friendly rivalry of sorts, but both Ohio and North Carolina claim to be the place where human flight first began. North Carolina has "First in Flight" on its license plates, commemorating the Wright Brothers' history-making flight at Kitty Hawk in 1903. Ohio had "Birthplace of Aviation" on its plates because the Wright Brothers were born and came up with the idea for their plane in Dayton. Ohio later changed their license-plate motto to "Birthplace of Aviation Pioneers" to include Neil Armstrong and John Glenn—both Ohio natives. So, in a sense, both states were first in flight.

Armstrong has been quoted as saying, "There's enough credit for both states—North Carolina provided the right winds and soft landing material, and Ohio provided the know-how and the resources."

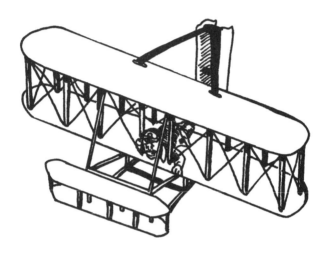

Conquest of the Air

The December 17, 1903, inaugural flight of the *Wright Flyer* will be forever immortalized near the location of the actual event. On March 2, 1927, Congress established the Kill Devil Hills Monument National Memorial in Manteo. The name was officially changed to the Wright Brothers National Monument on August 10, 1933. The monument is a 60-foot, triangular pylon made of gray granite from Mount Airy. It looks like a giant bird getting ready to take flight.

The inscription on the monument reads as follows:

In commemoration of the conquest of the air by the brothers Wilbur and Orville Wright conceived by Genius, achieved by Dauntless Resolution and Unconquerable Faith.

There are actual markers on the dune face where the *Wright Flyer* took off and landed on that historic day in 1903, as well as a reconstruction of the camp that the Wright Brothers used while doing their experiments. The monument is maintained by the National Park Service, as well as the North Carolina Department of Cultural Resources.

North Carolina NUGGET NASA astronaut Neil Armstrong took a small piece of the original wing covering of the *Wright Flyer* with him during the *Apollo 11* mission to the moon on July 20, 1969. What better way to honor the men who perfected winged flight?

Everybody Was Kitty Hawk Gliding…Hyah!

Up, up and away! The Kitty Hawk Kites (KHK) Flight School is the oldest hang-gliding school on the East Coast and the largest school of its kind in the world. It was founded in 1974 by John Harris, an industry pioneer, to help train and educate people in the blossoming sport of hang gliding. In the 1980s, KHK was providing flight training, selling kites and accessories and promoting outdoor recreation activities. The flight school takes full advantage of Jockey's Ridge—the tallest natural sand dune on the East Coast—for all its foot-powered glider launches. The KHK Flight School has trained over 300,000 people since its inception.

North Carolina NUGGET The late Dr. Francis Rogallo is credited with being the father of hang gliding. Rogallo invented the flexible-wing glider design in 1948, while working for the National Advisory Committee for Aeronautics (NACA). Rogallo was inducted into the North Carolina Sports Hall of Fame in 1987 and is memorialized at the Wright Brothers Memorial in Kitty Hawk. Rogallo passed away in Southern Shores on September 1, 2009.

NOTABLE EVENTS

Tar Heel Timeline

As one of the 13 original colonies, North Carolina has seen a plethora of historical happenings and notable events in its nearly 400 years of existence. Because of that, I decided that a timeline would be the best way to showcase some of NC's important dates, courtesy of the North Carolina Museum of History.

1587: The birth of Virginia Dare, the first child born to English parents in America

1663: Charles II issues the Carolina Charter—NC's "birth certificate"

1718: Blackbeard the pirate is killed near Ocracoke Inlet

1776: The Halifax Resolves are adopted—the first formal sanction of American independence

1789: North Carolina ratifies the Constitution

1789: The University of North Carolina receives its charter, making it the first state (and the nation's oldest) university

1839: The first public school law in North Carolina is passed

1856: The North Carolina Railroad is completed

1861: North Carolina secedes from the Union

1865: The Battle of Bentonville, the last major battle of the Civil War, takes place

1865: The last major Confederate army surrenders at Bennett House in present-day Durham County

1874: Reynolds and Duke establish tobacco factories

1898: The Wilmington Race Riot

1900: The North Carolina Literary and Historical Association is established

1903: The Wright brothers achieve powered flight

1921: The first commercial radio broadcast (WBT)

1948: The first commercial television broadcast (WBTV)

1958: Research Triangle Park is established

1960: The first lunch counter sit-in occurs in Greensboro

1962: Susie Sharp becomes the first woman on the North Carolina Supreme Court

1983: Henry E. Frye becomes the first African American on the North Carolina Supreme Court

1997: The governor obtains veto power

2008: Beverly E. Perdue becomes North Carolina's first female governor

2010: John V. Wood and Lisa Wojna write the *North Carolina Trivia* book

THE NAME GAME

Talk Like a Tar Heel

All across the country, there are town or county names that look easy to pronounce, but end up being harder than you think. That's an simple easy way for locals to look at you and say, "You're not from 'round here, are you?" North Carolina is no exception. Take a look at the list of towns and counties below.

☛ Cities and Towns

Ahoskie (*uh-HAHS-kee*)
Bahama (*ba-HEY-mah*)
Beaufort (*BOH-furt*)
Chickamacomico
  (*chick-uh-muh-CAH-mih-co*)
Conetoe (*ke-NEE-dah*)
Cullowhee (*CULL-uh-wee*)
Etowah (*EH-tuh-wuh*)
Fuquay-Varina
  (*FEW-kway vuh-REE-nuh*)
Icard (*EYE-kurd*)
Ijames (*IMES*)

Kerr Lake (*CAR*)
Lake Junaluska
  (*joon-uh-LUSK-uh*)
Lucama (*loo-CAH-muh*)
Mebane (*MEB-in*)
Pfafftown (*POFF-town*)
Potecasi (*POE-tuh-KAY-see*)
Rodanthe (*row-DAN-thee*)
Uwharrie (*you-WHAR-ee*)
Wendell (*win-DELL*)
Yeopim (*YOE-pim*)

☛ Counties

Alleghany (*al-i-GAINY*)
Bertie (*ber-TEE*)
Buncombe (*BUNK-um*)
Cabarrus (*ka-BARE-us*)
Harnett (*HARR-nit*)
Hertford (*HERT-ferd*)

Pasquotank (*PASS-kwa-tank*)
Perquimans (*per-QUIM-ans*)
Robeson (*ROBB-i-son*)
Rowan (*row-ANN*)
Tyrrell (*TERR-il*)
Watauga (*wah-TAW-gah*)

They Named a Town THAT?!?!

North Carolina has a penchant for the interesting town name and these are just a few of the weirdest ones (includes cities, towns, townships and communities):

Bandana	Frog Level	Kill Devil Hills
Bat Cave	Frog Pond	Little Switzerland
Black Jack	Frogsboro	Lizard Lick
Boogertown	Frying Pan	Luck
Bottom	Gum Neck	Meat Camp
Climax	Half Hell	Sunshine
Erect	Hog Island	Tick Bite
Fork	Horneytown	Whynot

Naughty, Naughty!

There's a saying that "you have to go through *Horneytown* to get to *High Point* and then on to *Climax*." Whew, is it getting hot in here?

Pretty Cool, Eh?

You can even find a Canada in North Carolina! It is located in the western part of the state, near Wolf Mountain and the Nantahala National Forest.

CLAIM TO FAME

Just Holler!

Long before text messaging and cellular phones, there was a great method of communicating across long distances in rural North Carolina—you just hollered at your neighbor. Every third Saturday in June in Spivey's Corner, people from around the country meet up in the quaint little town and holler for all they're worth. The National Hollerin' Contest is a worldwide phenomenon and has been since it started in 1969—thanks to an off-the-cuff comment made by contest co-founder Ermon Godwin on a radio program. Two-time hollerin' champion Kevin Jasper (2000, 2004) has been on *Late Night with David Letterman*, *Live with Regis and Kathie Lee* and hundreds of radio stations. Jasper believes it is his "privilege and responsibility to educate the public in the fine folk art of Spivey's Corner Hollerin'."

During the National Hollerin' Contest, there are also several other competitions that take place. There's the Conch Shell Blowin' Contest, the Junior Hollerin' Contest, the Teen Hollerin' Contest and the Ladies' Callin' Contest.

 Judges are picky about the hollerin' they hear in Spivey's Corner. You have to know the history of the four main hollers (distress, functional, communicative and expressive) and why you are hollerin'. It takes more than just a loud, booming voice. Yodel-ay-hee-hoo!

DID YOU  KNOW?

It is said that the modern police/fire/rescue siren sound is based on the distress holler. It is fitting, then, that this contest was originally a fundraiser for the Spivey's Corner Volunteer Fire Department.

Drop a 'Possum by the Tail

Raleigh drops a huge acorn on New Year's Eve because it's the City of Oaks. Well, Brasstown is considered to be the "Opossum Capital of the World," and guess what it drops on the last day of the year? That's right…an opossum. Clay Logan, the 'Possum Drop master of ceremonies, says on his website, "If New York can drop a ball, and Georgia can drop a peach, then we can lower the 'possum."

Johnston County also celebrates an animal once a year. The annual Mule Days celebration in Benson attracts enthusiasts from all over the state, and the county school system even gives the students a day off during the festivities.

Follow the Yellow Brick Road

We're off to see the wizard, the wonderful wizard of Beech Mountain! Wait, where's Oz? Or the Emerald City? The Land of Oz theme park was in full operation on Beech Mountain from 1970 until 1980, thanks to Tweetsie Railroad founder Grover Robbins and designer Jack Pentes. Vandals and collectors (or were they flying monkeys?) tarnished the park in the '80s, and it lost the luster the Emerald City once possessed. In the mid '90s, the Emerald Mountain Project began—volunteers unearthed the Yellow Brick Road and patched it up, and now they throw the biggest Wizard of Oz party this side of Kansas. The Autumn at Oz party in October brings "Ozzies" back together to walk the Yellow Brick Road, enjoy the manicured gardens and pay tribute to NC's own Emerald City. Proceeds from Autumn at Oz pay for the party and the continued restoration of the park.

DID YOU KNOW?

Dorothy's "house" at the theme park is actually a rental cabin for lovebirds and other people who want to "not be in Kansas anymore."

Let There Be Lights...and Lots of Them!

There is a small town on the South Fork River in Gaston County that puts Clark Griswold and *National Lampoon's Christmas Vacation* to shame. McAdenville, known internationally as Christmas Town USA, began decorating the live trees around town in 1956. Nearly 400 trees, ranging in height from six to 90 feet, were strung with lights in 2009. Homeowners decorate their front doors, and hundreds of wreaths adorn lightposts throughout town. There's even a life-sized nativity scene, a 46-foot-wide lighted image of Old Man Winter and fountains in the lake in the center of town shoot water 75 feet into the air.

DID YOU **KNOW?**

The McAdenville Christmas Lights celebration generates an estimated $11.8 million annually for the local economy, according to
the findings of a regional economic impact study in 2003. Approximately 600,000 visitors view the light pageantry in a typical season,
which lasts from December 1 to 26, with more than 75 percent
of the visitors coming from areas outside Gaston County.

CRUNCHING THE NUMBERS

That's Gross...

...but only if you hate money. North Carolina's gross state product (GSP) in 2008 was over $400 million ($400,192,000 to be exact). That amount was 10th nationally, down from ninth in 2007. Gross state product measures the total economic output of a state over a set period of time and is the state counterpart of the national gross domestic product (GDP). Add together all the value of the industrial assets in a state, and you've got yourself a GSP. Cool.

DID YOU  **KNOW?**

The state with the lowest GSP is Vermont, at just over $24 million. That's just six percent of North Carolina's GSP.

Penny for Your Thoughts

In 2008, Forbes.com ranked North Carolina the third-best state for doing business in the nation, the second consecutive year that the state held that ranking. Also, *Site Selection* magazine ranked the Tar Heel State as having the number-one business climate for five out of the last six years.

Breadwinners

The median annual income for a North Carolina household in 2008 was $46,549—just over $5000 lower than the national average of $52,029. For kicks and giggles, it's *only* $24,000 lower than the state with the highest median income—Maryland, with $70,545.

Home Sweet Home

Across the entire state, the estimated median home value in 2008 was $154,500. In 2008, the mean price for all home units was $281,969. To break it down even further:

☛ Detached house: $309,212

☛ Townhouses or other attached unit: $200,632

☛ In a two-unit structure: $400,000

☛ In a three-to-four-unit structure: $135,312

☛ In a five-or-more-unit structure: $149,119

☛ Mobile home: $31,954

PLANES, TRAINS AND AUTOMOBILES!

Into the Wild Blue Yonder

North Carolinians sure love to fly. According to the NC Division of Aviation, the state has 74 publicly owned airports and nearly 300 privately owned ones. Nine airports have regularly scheduled airline service, and four are international: Raleigh-Durham International, Charlotte-Douglas International, Wilmington International and Piedmont Triad International. More than 47 million passengers fly to and from the Tar Heel State yearly, and over 800 million pounds of airfreight leave the state each year. Up, up and away…

Keeping the State on Track

North Carolina has 3684 miles of railroad tracks throughout the state—more than the distance between Wilmington, North Carolina, and Los Angeles, California, in case you were wondering. The two main Amtrak local trains are the *Piedmont* (trains 73 and 76) and the *Carolinian* (trains 79 and 80).

The *Piedmont* stays inside the state's borders, traveling between Charlotte and Raleigh twice daily. The *Carolinian* travels between Charlotte and New York City. Combined, the *Carolinian* and the *Piedmont* carry more than 200,000 passengers each year.

Off the Beaten Track

Two major freight railroad companies operate in North Carolina—CSX Transportation and Norfolk Southern. Also, there are more than 20 smaller freight railroads, known as "shortlines."

The Short and Long of It

The state's first railroad was built in 1833 and was called the "Experimental Railroad." (Creative name, isn't it?) It was used to carry rock needed to build the state capitol in Raleigh. It was less than two miles long, so I guess this was also the state's first "shortline." Also, NC can boast that it had the world's longest railroad at one point—one very short point—when the Wilmington to Weldon railroad was completed in March 1840. It was 161.5 miles long.

North Carolina NUGGET Governor Perdue announced in January 2010 that North Carolina had received $545 million to help build a high-speed rail line between Charlotte, North Carolina, and Washington, DC, with trains traveling at speeds of 90 to 110 miles per hour. Sounds like me driving to DC on I-85. Ahem…yeah…moving on…

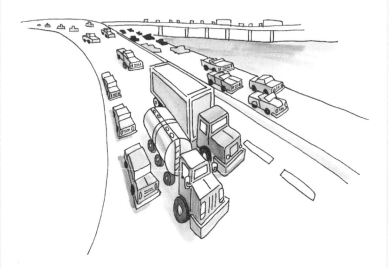

On the Road Again…

North Carolina has the nation's second largest highway network, with over 98,000 highway miles and six interstates. Texas has the largest, in case you were wondering.

North Carolina NUGGET The middle section of I-40 is sometimes loosely called the "Tobacco Road" because it is the major connector between NC State, Duke, UNC-Chapel Hill and Wake Forest universities. All four schools are less than 10 miles from I-40.

DID YOU KNOW?

"Tobacco Road" was also a hit song across several musical genres, recorded first by John D. Loudermilk (1960), then The Nashville Teens (1964) and Lou Rawls (1966), to name just a few.

The Mother of Good Roads

Growing up in North Carolina, I heard several stories about NC being called the "Good Roads State." If it wasn't for Chapel Hill resident Harriet Morehead Berry, it probably never would have been an issue. In 1904, Berry was appointed secretary of the NC Geological and Economic Survey committee and helped coordinate the Good Roads Association. Berry worked for 20 years to bring North Carolina "out of the mud" (most of the roads in the state were unpaved at the time, obviously), until the Good Roads Bill was finally passed in 1921. The bill provided $50 million to pave, construct and maintain the state's highway system. How was Berry thanked for her hard work? She was removed from the state Geological and Economic Survey, but she continued to serve the state in various other ways until her death in 1940.

GOT TO BE NC AGRICULTURE

Farming the Numbers

North Carolina is an agricultural powerhouse and has been as long as I can remember. I grew up on a very large tobacco, corn, soybean and winter wheat farm in Clayton (Johnston County), and the land is still being farmed today. In 2008, the state ranked in the top five of several agricultural exports:

Rank	Item	Production	NC % of U.S.
1	All tobacco	390.4 (million lbs)	48.8
1	Flue-cured tobacco	384.75 (million lbs)	77.1

1	Sweet potatoes	8740 (cwt)	47.4
2	Christmas trees	100 (million $)	23.9
2	Hogs and pigs	9.7 (million head)	14.4
2	Turkeys	40 (million head)	14.6
3	Cucumbers, processed	42.3 (tons)	7.5
3	Trout sold (foodsize)	3.55 (million lbs)	6.8
4	Cucumbers, fresh market	735 (cwt)	7.4
4	Strawberries	208 (cwt)	0.8
5	Broilers	796.1 (million head)	8.8
5	Burley tobacco	5.6 (million lbs)	2.8
5	Cotton	755 (bales)	5.9
5	Greenhouse and nursery	777 (million $)	4.8
5	Peanuts	358.9 (million lbs)	7.0

High Five

The top five cash receipts from farming by commodity in 2008 (in thousands of dollars) were as follows:

1. Broilers	$2,691,619
2. Hogs	$2,170,806
3. Greenhouse/Nursery/Christmas trees	$777,183
4. Tobacco	$686,833
5. Turkeys	$652,320

I Yam What I Yam...

People have been confusing sweet potatoes and yams for the longest time. It all began when Africans were brought to the New World to be used as slaves. The yam, which is a staple of most African diets, looks a little bit like a sweet potato. The African word for yam is *nyami*. See the similarity? Many slaves used the words yam and "sweet potato" synonymously, and the name stuck. The garnet and jewel varieties of "yams" are actually sweet potatoes with a moist, orange flesh. The U.S. Department of Agriculture requires that the label "yam" always be accompanied by "sweet potato," to avoid any unnecessary confusion.

DID YOU KNOW?

The most popular moist-fleshed sweet potato varieties grown in North Carolina include the Covington, Beauregard, Hernandez, Jewel, Puerto Rico, Japanese, O'Henry and White Delight.

 The small town of Smithfield actually holds an annual Ham & Yam Festival on the first weekend of May. It started in 1984 as a challenge from Johnston County pig farmers to the "foreign" pig farmers of Smithfield, Virginia. The event features cooking contests for both hams and yams, as well as agricultural exhibits, live music, and arts and crafts booths.

Smoke 'Em If You Got 'Em

Tobacco and North Carolina have been synonymous since the 19th century. Washington Duke built his first tobacco factory in 1874. In 1881, his son, James Buchanan "Buck" Duke, entered the manufactured cigarette business in Durham. His first cigarette was the Duke of Durham brand. The Duke

factory produced 9.8 million cigarettes that year, which was 1.5 percent of the total market at the time. Buck Duke later started the American Tobacco Company in 1884 and was also a major benefactor of Trinity College, which later became Duke University (didn't see that coming, did you?).

OTHER ECONOMIC MOTHER LODES

If You Build It...

When it comes to textile production, North Carolina is a world leader. According to the NC Department of Commerce, the state's growth as a center for textile manufacturers has garnered these accolades:

- ☛ The state is home to over 1500 textile-complex facilities that employ over 180,000 people with a $2.8 billion payroll.

- ☛ Of these companies, 185 have their headquarters in North Carolina.

- ☛ The industry earns over $35 billion in annual revenues.

☞ Since 2003, there have been 144 new or expanded textile operations.

☞ North Carolina is the number-one textile mill employer in the nation.

☞ It is also the number-one non-woven roll goods producer in the nation.

☞ The state is the number-four apparel producer in the nation.

☞ North Carolina is also the number-one yarn producer in the nation, with many of the world's largest companies located in the state.

☞ It is also home to four of the top five suppliers of home textiles.

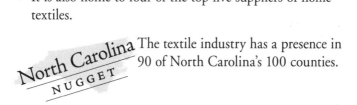 The textile industry has a presence in 90 of North Carolina's 100 counties.

DID YOU KNOW?

North Carolina State University in Raleigh and Clemson University in Clemson, South Carolina, have two of the best textile schools in the world. When they meet on the gridiron during a hard-fought Atlantic Coast Conference football game, it's called the "Textile Bowl," as it has been since 1981.

Textile Mastery

With over 107 years of teaching, research and extension, the NC State University College of Textiles is the leading textile college in the world. The college is located in a 300,000-square-foot, state-of-the-art facility on the 1334-acre Centennial Campus. And I'm not just spinning a yarn. Get it? Spinning a *yarn*? Oh well, never mind…

The first cotton mill in the state was the Schenck-Warlick mill, which opened in 1814 near Lincolnton.

Soldiering On...

North Carolina has the fourth largest military presence of any state in the nation. The largest U.S. Army base is located in Fayetteville–Fort Bragg. Combined with nearby Pope Air Force Base, the tandem forms one of the largest military bases of operation in the world. That being said, the defense industry is a large part of North Carolina's economic structure. Seven of the 10 largest global air defense companies have operations in North Carolina including Boeing, General Dynamics, GE, L-3 Communications, Lockheed Martin, Northrup Grumman and Raytheon.

Dressed for Success
In 2005, the U.S. Department of Defense invested almost $156 million in North Carolina, buying textile products for all branches of the military.

 It is fitting that the aerospace and aviation industry has a big presence in North Carolina. Orville and Wilbur Wright, the Fathers of Flight, would take all the credit, I'm sure.

DID YOU KNOW?

Fort Bragg started in 1918 as Camp Bragg—a temporary field-artillery site named for Civil War Confederate general Braxton Bragg. It did not receive permanent "Fort" status until 1922.

GENERAL HEALTH AND WELLNESS

With This Ring, I Promise...

For the last few decades, North Carolina has been below the national average as far as marriage rates are concerned. In 1988, the national marriage rate average was slightly less than 10 marriages per 1000 population, and North Carolina sat right at eight per 1000. Something happened in 1998 and 2000, because those were the only two out the last 20 years that the state topped the U.S. average. There were 64,308 couples who tied the knot across North Carolina in 2008.

D-I-V-O-R-C-E

Tammy Wynette's song "D-I-V-O-R-C-E" rings true to anyone who has seen their marriage come and go. North Carolinians may be below the marriage national average, but they've been above the national divorce average since 1988. Over the last 20 years, the average divorce rate has fluctuated between 4.0 and 5.0 per 1000 population—nationally, it's stayed between 3.8 and 4.2 per 1000. In 2008, there were 35,618 divorces or annulments in the state.

That's Life!

According to research conducted between 1996 and 2000 by Paul A. Buescher and Ziya Gizlice, the average life expectancy in North Carolina is 75.6 years. But that number fluctuates slightly between males and females, and between Caucasians and people of color:

☞ White females can expect to live about 79.6 years.

☞ White males don't fare quite as well, with an average life expectancy of 73.8 years.

☛ Minority males have a significantly shorter average life expectancy of 68 years.

☛ Minority females don't fare quite as well as their white counterparts, but outdo minority males with a 75.8-year life expectancy.

We're Having a Baby!
In 2008, there were 130,758 live births in the state (67,038 males and 63,720 females). Out of that total, 54,952 were born out of wedlock.

DID YOU KNOW?

Between 2000 and 2006, there were 749,959 births and 456,198 deaths in North Carolina.

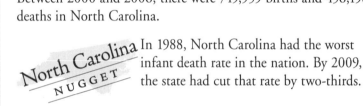

In 1988, North Carolina had the worst infant death rate in the nation. By 2009, the state had cut that rate by two-thirds.

Only You Can Prevent...
As far as preventable causes of death are concerned, the highest-ranking ones in 2007 should be no surprise to North Carolinians. Tobacco use (13,720), physical inactivity (12,583) and alcohol consumption (2653) were the top three.

DID YOU KNOW?

Heart disease, cancer, stroke and chronic lung disease are the leading causes of death in North Carolina.

"Caring" About You

In 2008, 1,404,787 North Carolinians were enrolled in the Medicare program, which was 15.2 percent of the state's total population. In 2009, 1,450,104 were enrolled.

Papa Don't Preach...

North Carolina has the ninth highest teen pregnancy rate in the nation, with 58.6 pregnancies per 1000 teens aged 15 to 19 getting pregnant in 2008—a total of 19,398. Of those teen pregnancies, 5512 (28.4 percent) were repeats. Also in 2008, 376 girls aged 10 to 14 became pregnant (1.3 per 1000), which was a slight drop from 2007. Cumberland County had the highest number of teen pregnancies in 2008 (892), but Tyrrell County had the worst rate (116.1 per 1000)—even though they only had 13 teen pregnancies. Of the more than 19,000 reported resident teen pregnancies in 2007, 77 percent resulted in live births, 23 percent were aborted and less than one percent resulted in fetal death.

Getting Better

In 1990, the teen pregnancy rate in North Carolina was 105.4 per 1000 teenagers. Yikes! In 18 years, the rate has been cut almost in half (58.6 per 1000 in 2008).

Getting Busy

Sexually transmitted diseases are hard to control, regardless of what state you're in. North Carolina is no exception. In 2007, the state had the sixth highest gonorrhea rate (118.9 cases per 100,000 population), the 15th highest primary/secondary syphilis rate (3.7 per 100,000) and the 25th highest chlamydia rate (345.6 new infection cases per 100,000) in the United States. However, North Carolina has been very aggressive in trying to control these sexually transmitted diseases. With programs such as the NC Syphilis Elimination Project, the syphilis rate dropped 90 percent from 1992 (36.2 cases per 100,000 population) to 2007 (3.8 cases per 100,000 population).

A Growing Problem

The average number of North Carolinians who are overweight or obese has increased steadily since 1990, right along with the national average. In 1990, 12.9 percent of Tar Heel residents were obese, compared to 11.6 nationally. Just like Morgan Spurlock in the documentary *Super Size Me*, North Carolina added several notches to its leather belt. In 2007, 28.7 percent of the state (as compared to 26.3 nationally) was considered obese.

DRUGS, BOOZE AND ALL THINGS NAUGHTY

What's Your Drug of Choice?
According to the U.S. Drug Enforcement Administration (DEA), North Carolina is considered a secondary regional drug distribution hub. Huh? What that means is that because of our extensive transportation network (highways and interstates), it is easy to move drugs through the state. The DEA also sees a direct correlation between the drug trafficking problem and the influx of foreign nationals to the state.

In 2008, DEA officials seized 384 kilograms (847 pounds) of cocaine, 14.6 kilograms (32 pounds) of heroin, 19.2 kilograms (42 pounds) of methamphetamine and 5.1 kilograms (11 pounds) of hashish. There were 196 reported meth lab incidents across the state as well.

Bluntly Speaking…

Marijuana is one of the most prevalent drugs across North Carolina. DEA officials seized 1805.7 kilograms (3980 pounds) of marijuana during raids in 2008. In 2005, marijuana was the state's number-five cash crop. Nearly 5000 marijuana plants were either seized or destroyed from public lands this year, mostly in the northern region of the state near the Appalachian Mountains.

In January 2010, detectives in Kinston uncovered a buried (yes, buried) school bus full of Mary Jane. A drug dog fell through a disguised trapdoor, which led to the discovery. Police seized 68 plants, worth about $40,000. Each plant weighed over 30 pounds and was roughly four feet tall. I guess you really could call that a "bust." Or would that be "bussed?"

Moonshine

Ever wondered why corn whiskey distilled illegally got the name "moonshine"? Well, legend has it that people made it under the cover of darkness—under the light of the moon, so to speak—to avoid getting caught. The only ingredients you need to make moonshine are cornmeal, sugar, water, yeast and malt. Getting the still is the hard part. And make sure you heat the mash to at least 173°F. Otherwise, you've got some spoiled moonshine, and nobody likes a wasted batch.

Moonshine has a storied history throughout North Carolina. From the revenuers in the Appalachians to bootleggers running two steps ahead of the Highway Patrol, moonshine has and will always be a part of the state's rural heritage. When I was a boy, I heard stories of a store nearby that sold "samples" of moonshine in mason jars. My dad always told me to stay away from the stuff, because it "would put hair in places you didn't care to have." That description sounded so appealing to a 14-year-old…not.

A Glass By Any Other Name

Moonshine has gone by several names over the years, and most parts of the state have their own name for it. Here's a list of the most popular ones:

bush whiskey	ruckus juice
catdaddy	skull cracker
corn liquor	'splo
galley bourbon	stump
hillbilly pop	stumphole
mule kick	sugar whiskey
panther's breath	tiger's sweat
rotgut	white lightning

North Carolina NUGGET It's been said that good moonshine will "make a mouse bite off a tomcat's tail," or maybe even "make a rabbit whip a bulldog." Grab yourself a jar and find out.

DID YOU KNOW?

NASCAR owner Junior Johnson is part owner of the only legitimate moonshine distillery in the state. Piedmont Distillers, Inc. operates out of a 1915 train station in the Blue Ridge Mountain town of Madison and has been producing Cat Daddy and Midnight Moon moonshine out of an authentic, small-batch copper pot since 2005.

The Grapes of Non-Wrath

Since the scuppernong is North Carolina's official fruit, it makes sense that the state is also one of the biggest wine producers in the United States (eighth in wine production, ninth in grape production). The state is home to close to 90 wineries, and that number has quadrupled since 2001 according to the North Carolina Department of Commerce. Duplin Winery in Rose Hill is the world's leading producer of muscadine (scuppernong) wine and is also the largest and oldest winery in North Carolina.

DID YOU KNOW?

The most-visited winery in the United States is in Asheville. The historic Biltmore Winery receives more than a million visitors each year.

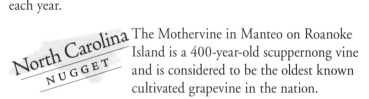

The Mothervine in Manteo on Roanoke Island is a 400-year-old scuppernong vine and is considered to be the oldest known cultivated grapevine in the nation.

Be "Free" in NC

Believe it or not, there are several clothing-optional opportunities in the Tar Heel State. One of the better choices is the Jasmine Trail Nudist Resort and Campground, located just a few miles away from Tryon Palace in New Bern. A proud member of the American Association for Nude Recreation (AANR), Jasmine Trail walked away with two awards in 2008—both for the largest membership increase.

Another option is Whispering Pines Nudist Resort, located on Ocean Isle Beach, just south of Wilmington. For a non-beach option, the Triangle Area Nudists (TAN, which I find hilarious) in the Research Triangle Park area or the Bar-S Ranch in Reidsville might suit your fancy. Bring a towel, anyway.

Adam and Steve

A strong contingent of North Carolina voters lobbied the state legislature to amend the NC Constitution to prohibit same-sex marriages. According to a 2009 NC Civitas Institute poll, 76 percent of 600 registered state voters surveyed want to outlaw gay marriage, while only 21 percent support it. Several representatives got together and filed Senate Bill 272 during the 2009 legislative session. The bill states that the following should be added to Article 14, Section 6 of the state Constitution: "marriage between a man and a woman is the only domestic legal union that shall be valid or recognized in this State." The bill has been referred and will be picked up during the 2010 session.

DID YOU KNOW?

Joe Hertzenberg was the first openly gay elected official in North Carolina, serving on the Chapel Hill City Council from 1987 until 1993. He died in 2007 after complications from diabetes.

WTF?
In June 2008, the North Carolina Department of Motor Vehicles notified 10,000 license plate holders that the DMV would replace their current tag with a new one for free. OMG! Why would the DMV do that? Well, the offending plates had the acronym "WTF" on them. Ask your teenage son or daughter what it means. Srsly. That's how a 60-year-old technology teacher from Fayetteville found out and alerted the DMV in the first place. Kthxbai.

BEST IN BARBECUE

"Cue" the Fight Scene!

First of all, as has been said previously, "barbecue" is a noun or an adjective, *not* a verb. North Carolina barbecue focuses on the slow cooking of pork until fork tender, usually over hickory wood or some other smoky substance. Not only is North Carolina embroiled in a barbecue supremacy battle with areas such as Memphis, Tennessee, and Kansas City, Missouri, but we're also even fighting among ourselves! In all my years as a North Carolinian, I have found very few people that like and support both eastern-style *and* western-style 'cue.

DID YOU  KNOW?

The phrase "high on the hog" refers to either eating the better quality parts of a pig near the front of the animal (pork shoulder) or eating and living well in general.

What's the Difference?

Eastern-Style Barbecue	Western-Style (Lexington) Barbecue
Whole hog	Primarily pork shoulder
Vinegar-based sauce	Vinegar-based "dip" with tomatoes added
Hot/mild peppers and spices	Brown sugar and spices
Served with sweet coleslaw	Served with "red" slaw (BBQ slaw)
Corn sticks	Hushpuppies
Sweet tea	Sweet tea

Hog Heaven

Barbecue can be pulled, minced, chopped, coarse chopped (blocked) or sliced (sounds like a Waffle House menu choice). You can cook barbecue in a ground pit, a raised pit or a smoker. A pig pick'n is where a whole pig is cooked in a smoker and each person pulls the barbecue off by hand or a pit master does it and serves it gladly. I remember as a kid staring at the face of the dead pig as I pulled off a big hunk of 'cue at a pig pick'n. It was slightly creepy, but the taste was well worth it.

 Two phrases are used in reference to the making of eastern-style barbecue:

☞ We use every part of the pig except the squeal!

☞ We use the whole pig—from the rooter to the tooter! (Think about it.)

OLDEST SCHOOLS

Gotta Start Somewhere
The University of North Carolina at Chapel Hill is the nation's oldest public university. People here refer to the university as either UNC or Carolina. The university opened its doors to students on January 15, 1795, and received its first student, Hinton James of New Hanover County, on February 12 of that year. Carolina is also the only public university in the nation to graduate a student in the 18th century.

DID YOU KNOW?

In 1898, Sallie Walker Stockard did something no other woman had done up until then. She became the first woman to graduate from the University of North Carolina.

In My Mind, I'm Goin' to Carolina...

James Taylor penned those words in the 1968 song "Carolina in My Mind." Taylor grew up in Carrboro—a stone's throw from the majestic university. The song opines about Taylor's desire to return back to the state he called home for so many years. Taylor wrote the song while in London, England, recording for Apple Records. UNC fans have often used the song as their unofficial motto, and some even consider it the unofficial state song.

DID YOU KNOW?

The first building constructed on UNC's campus, the Old East building, is now listed as a National Historic Landmark. The two-story brick building was the only structure on campus for the first two years of operation and is still in use today as a dormitory. The day that the first cornerstone for Old East was laid—October 12, 1793—is now known as University Day, or simply UNC's birthday.

 Charles Griffin (1679–1720) was the first professional educator on record in the colony now known as North Carolina. In 1705, he established a school near Symond's Creek, eight miles south of what is now Elizabeth City, and it is believed to have been the first school of any kind in the state.

Humble Beginnings

Nestled in Franklin County, Louisburg College is the nation's oldest two-year institution. The state's only residential two-year program, Louisburg College started off in two phases: Franklin Male Academy opened on January 1, 1805, and the Louisburg Women's Academy opened on December 27, 1814.

DID YOU KNOW?

The Franklin Male Academy began under the direction of Yale graduate Matthew Dickinson, who was qualified to teach more than 20 subjects, including five languages.

NORTH CAROLINA'S PUBLIC SCHOOLS

The Numbers Keep Growing

North Carolina's K-12 student population has consistently grown year after year because of the influx of people moving into the state. With NC being a great place to start a business or raise a family, the word is getting out. During the 2003–04 school year, the total number of students in the public school system (not including charter schools) was 1,374,887, with the highest single-grade total being ninth grade (126,888). During 2007–08, the number jumped to 1,458,156 students, with the freshman year in high school having the highest total again (135,693). No wonder my ninth-grade English classes keep getting bigger and bigger—I thought it was just me.

Drilling into the Numbers

Out of the total population for the 2007–08 school year, here's the gender and race breakdown:

☞ **Native American:** 10,355 males, 10,023 females

☞ **Asian:** 17,639 males, 17,501 females

☞ **Hispanic:** 77,995 males, 74,610 females

☞ **Black:** 224,463 males, 220,407 females

☞ **White:** 398,268 males, 376,699 females

Student Populations by County

Robeson County had the highest Native American student numbers of any county, partly because of the high Lumbee Indian population in that neck of the woods. In 2007–08, Robeson County enrolled 5336 males and 5050 females of Native American heritage.

Wake County had the highest Asian (3991 males, 3962 females) and white (36,434 males, 34,848 females) enrollment, while Charlotte-Mecklenburg schools had the highest Hispanic (10,511 males, 10,298 females) and black (30,342 males, 30,751 females) enrollment.

To Go, or Not to Go

North Carolina is home to the oldest four-year university and oldest two-year college in the nation, so higher education has always been a draw for graduating high school seniors. But what about the ones who decide to do something else?

In 2008, 3.5 percent of high school seniors (2904) entered the military, and 8.1 percent (6749) directly entered the workforce.

Home Base

North Carolina's home school numbers continue to rise as well, with a reported 41,042 homeschool sites across the state in 2008. Of that number, 13,979 (34.1 percent) were independent and 27,063 (65.9 percent) were religious in nature. A total of 77,065 students were homeschooled in 2008.

DID YOU KNOW?

In 1989, there were only 1385 homeschool locations across the state, serving a total of 2325 students.

Homeschooling by County

The 10 counties with the highest homeschool sites in 2008:

☛ **Wake:** 3771 sites (7571 students)

☛ **Mecklenburg:** 2956 sites (6296 students)

☛ **Buncombe:** 1637 sites (2921 students)

☛ **Guilford:** 1568 sites (2940 students)

- **Union:** 1373 sites (2746 students)

- **Forsyth:** 1321 sites (2476 students)

- **Cumberland:** 1217 sites (2141 students)

- **Cabarrus:** 924 sites (1740 students)

- **Davidson:** 866 sites (1500 students)

- **Iredell:** 862 sites (1499 students)

North Carolina NUGGET The county with the smallest number of reported homeschool sites in 2008 was Tyrrell County. They had a whopping 22 registered locations, with a total of 27 students.

HIGHER LEARNING

The UNC System

The University of North Carolina system is a collection of 16 institutions across the state:

☞ Appalachian State University (Boone)

☞ East Carolina University (Greenville)

☞ Elizabeth City State University (Elizabeth City)

☞ Fayetteville State University (Fayetteville)

☛ North Carolina Agricultural & Technical University (Greensboro)

☛ North Carolina Central University (Durham)

☛ North Carolina State University (Raleigh)

☛ University of North Carolina at Asheville

☛ University of North Carolina at Chapel Hill

☛ University of North Carolina at Charlotte

☛ University of North Carolina at Greensboro

☛ University of North Carolina at Pembroke

☛ University of North Carolina at Wilmington

☛ University of North Carolina School of the Arts (Winston-Salem)

☛ Western Carolina University (Cullowhee)

☛ Winston-Salem State University (Winston-Salem)

North Carolina NUGGET The UNC System also includes the North Carolina School of Science and Mathematics (NCSSM) in Durham. NCSSM opened its doors in 1980 and was the first public residential high school in the nation for gifted students. Founded by former Governor James B. Hunt Jr., NCSSM educates academically and intellectually gifted high school juniors and seniors from every corner of the state and hundreds more through online learning and distance education.

DID YOU KNOW?

Keep hope alive! Reverend Jesse Jackson graduated from North Carolina's A&T University in 1964.

Lazy Sunday
Saturday Night Live's Chris Parnell, known for his *SNL* "shorts" with fellow comedian Andy Samberg, received his bachelor of fine arts degree from the NC School of the Arts.

What's Your Major?

Across the entire UNC system, the top 10 most popular degrees conferred in 2009 were as follows:

☞ Business Administration and Management, General: 2178

☞ Psychology, General: 1903

☞ Nursing, Registered Nurse Training (RN, ASN, BSN, MSN): 1692

☞ Biology/Biological Sciences, General: 1449

☞ Elementary Education and Teaching: 1439

☞ Communication Studies/Speech Communication and Rhetoric: 999

☞ Political Science and Government, General: 969

☞ Criminal Justice/Safety Studies: 909

☞ English Language and Literature, General: 842

☞ Accounting: 739

Private Universities
There are 36 independent colleges and universities located across North Carolina offering 126 different bachelor's or associate's degrees. I attended two of them (Wake Forest and Campbell), and of the over 80,000 students who enroll every year, more than half are North Carolinians. Independent colleges and universities grant almost one-third of the baccalaureate degrees awarded each year in North Carolina, about 45 percent of the medical degrees and more than 60 percent of the law degrees.

DID YOU KNOW?

Many people wonder why Wake Forest University is not in Wake Forest. Well, it used to be. The Z. Smith Reynolds Foundation gave generously to the university, and in 1956, WFU agreed to move to Winston-Salem—the home of the R.J. Reynolds Tobacco Company.

The Dean's List
Below is a list of the independent colleges and universities in the Tar Heel State:

☞ Barton College (Wilson)

☞ Belmont Abbey College (Belmont)

☞ Bennett College for Women (Greensboro)

☞ Brevard College (Brevard)

☞ Cabarrus College of Health Sciences (Concord)

☞ Campbell University (Buies Creek)

☞ Catawba College (Salisbury)

☞ Chowan University (Murfreesboro)

☞ Davidson College (Davidson)

☞ Duke University (Durham)

☞ Elon University (Greensboro)

☞ Gardner-Webb University (Boiling Springs)

☞ Greensboro College (Greensboro)

☞ Guilford College (Greensboro)

☞ High Point University (High Point)

- Johnson C. Smith University (Charlotte)

- Lees-McRae College (Banner Elk)

- Lenoir-Rhyne University (Hickory)

- Livingstone College (Salisbury)

- Louisburg College (Louisburg)

- Mars Hill College (Mars Hill)

- Meredith College (Raleigh)

- Methodist University (Fayetteville)

- Montreat College (Montreat)

- Mount Olive College (Mt. Olive)

- North Carolina Wesleyan College (Rocky Mount)

- Peace College (Raleigh)

- Pfeiffer University (Misenheimer)

- Queens University of Charlotte (Charlotte)

- St. Andrews Presbyterian College (Laurinburg)

- Saint Augustine's College (Raleigh)

- Salem College (Winston-Salem)

- Shaw University (Raleigh)

- Wake Forest University (Winston-Salem)

- Warren Wilson College (Asheville)

- Wingate University (Wingate)

 Established in 1837 by the Religious Society of Friends (the Quakers), Guilford College is the third-oldest coed institution in the country.

DID YOU KNOW?

Belmont Abbey College is the state's only Catholic college, founded in 1876 by the Order of Saint Benedict.

Almost a Mile High...

Nestled between Beech Mountain, Sugar Mountain and Grandfather Mountain at somewhere near 4000 feet above sea level, Lees-McRae College has the highest elevation of any campus in the eastern United States.

DID YOU KNOW?

President Woodrow Wilson attended Davidson College as a freshman in 1874 but studied for only one year. Wilson officially withdrew because of ill health, but some stories suggest that he might have been expelled. College records prove that if he was expelled, it wasn't because of his grades—he was a solid student (except in math).

Show Me the Money!

The average tuition charged by the independent colleges and universities across North Carolina is 17 percent below the national average. That's not a bad deal!

 Carroll O'Connor, known to millions as the grumpy Archie Bunker from the hit television series *All in the Family*, attended Wake Forest College for three semesters beginning in 1941, eventually transferring to the University of Montana after World War II.

Community Colleges
The Tar Heel State boasts the third-largest community college system in the nation. During the 2006–07 school year, more than 809,000 students were enrolled at the 58 community colleges. More than 95 percent of them are in-state residents who will remain and work in the state after graduation, contributing directly to the state's tax base.

 There is a community college located within 30 minutes of 99 percent of the state's entire population.

Age Is Just a Number
The average age of a community college student is 32, with curriculum students being slightly younger than continuing education students.

What's in Your Salad Bowl?
It's not the "melting pot" anymore...unless you're looking for a good fondue restaurant in Raleigh. In the community college world, about 63 percent of curriculum students are women. Digging a little deeper, about two-thirds of curriculum students are white, one-fourth of the students are African American and 3.4 percent of curriculum students are Hispanic.

DID YOU KNOW?

The state's community college system has an educational agreement in place that designates specific courses for mandatory transfer credit to all statewide public four-year institutions.

NOTABLE PEOPLE AND EVENTS

The "Education Governor"

Charles B. Aycock, born in Goldsboro in 1859, was governor of North Carolina from 1901 to 1905. During that time, he increased state educational funding, built hundreds of schools, raised teacher salaries and established longer school terms. Aycock also supported education for people with mental illness, the mentally challenged, the deaf and the blind, and he increased state funding for specialized institutions. He also fought to give blacks a fair shake at an education, even though he was a strong supporter of segregation.

Aycock's home still stands, as a monument to the man who changed the face of education in North Carolina. Fittingly, a high school was named after him in his hometown of Goldsboro—C.B. Aycock High School, home of the Falcons.

DID YOU KNOW?

Before becoming governor, Aycock took part in the Wilmington Race Riot of 1898—believed to be the first and only coup d'état on American soil.

North Carolina NUGGET Richard M. Nixon, 37th president of the United States, graduated from Duke University's School of Law in 1937 and was president of the Duke Bar Association from 1936 to 1937.

The Hunt for Blue November

James B. Hunt is North Carolina's longest serving governor, being elected to four terms. He served from 1977 to 1985 and again from 1993 to 2001. During his Democratic political career, Hunt was a major supporter of public education, garnering national attention for NC's Smart Start program for pre-kindergarten students.

Always at the forefront of the educational stratosphere, Hunt was part of the Carnegie Task Force that created the National Board of Professional Teaching Standards. When your teacher spouse goes into hiding during the months of September through March while he or she works on their National Boards box, you can thank Governor Hunt (hey, the 12 percent pay increase for teachers is worth the headache).

Hunt High School is named after the former governor and is located in his hometown of Wilson. Speaking of high schools, I attended Clayton High School and Wake Forest University with Hunt's niece, Sarah.

DID YOU  KNOW?

James B. Hunt was, at one time, rumored to be Barack Obama's choice for Secretary of Education.

 Governor Hunt had a hand in creating the North Carolina Center for the Advancement of Teaching (NCCAT), when the state legislature chartered it in Cullowhee in 1985. He took the idea from Jean Powell, NC's Teacher of the Year in 1983, when she came to speak at an education commission hearing. My wife said that you are treated like education royalty while you're there and that the food is outstanding.

The Science of Education

There is a dorm at the North Carolina School of Science and Mathematics named after Hunt because he helped create the Durham high school—the first residential high school for science, technology, engineering and mathematics (STEM) education in the nation. Hunt also spearheaded the creation of the NC Biotechnology Center in 1981.

North Carolina NUGGET William L. Poteat, a biology professor at Wake Forest College in 1883, is credited with introducing the laboratory method of teaching biology. Up to this point, biology was primarily a recitation course in the South.

Other Notable NC Educators

☞ **Charlotte Hawkins Brown:** Born in Henderson, Dr. Brown founded the Palmer Institute, a rural school for African Americans, near Greensboro in 1902. The school served as a successful private school for more than 60 years. Brown is also known as the "First Lady of Social Graces."

☞ **William C. Friday:** President of the UNC system for 30 years, he is the namesake, along with his wife, of the William and Ida Friday Center for Continuing Education (UNC), as well as the Friday Institute for Educational Innovation (NC State).

☞ **Nathan Carter Newbold:** Newbold worked to raise grants and financial appropriations for new all-black colleges and schools. He was also the North Carolina Director of Negro Education.

☞ **Sequoyah:** Credited as the inventor of the Cherokee alphabet, Sequoyah spent a lot of his life in the North Carolina mountains. Born around 1766 to an English fur-trading father and a Cherokee mother, Sequoyah's non-Cherokee name was George Gist.

☞ **Charles D. McIver:** A long-time teacher and crusader for women's education, McIver founded the State Normal and Industrial School for Girls (now UNC-Greensboro) in 1891. This was the first college for women in North Carolina.

☞ **W.L. Moore:** The first headmaster and inaugural member of the board of trustees at Croatan Indian Normal School (now UNC-Pembroke), a school to help educate Native American students.

☞ **Archibald D. Murphey:** Known as the "Father of North Carolina Public Schools," Murphey is remembered for his proposals regarding a publicly financed system of education, as well as constitutional reform.

☞ **John Motley Morehead:** Building upon Murphey's proposal regarding a school for the hearing impaired, Morehead opened the North Carolina School for the Deaf in 1844 (now known as the Governor Morehead School). The Morehead Scholarship, a full ride to UNC-Chapel Hill, is named after him.

☞ **Oscar R. Sampson:** One of the first Lumbee students at Croatan Normal School (now UNC-Pembroke), Sampson served as chairman of UNCP's board of trustees for 32 years and taught at the university for 40 years.

☞ **Calvin H. Wiley:** As North Carolina's first superintendent of public schools (1853–65), Wiley restored the public's faith in the state's educational system through his extensive public instruction reform.

DID YOU KNOW?

Elizabeth Duncan Koontz, the first black president of the National Education Association (NEA) was a Salisbury native.

North Carolina NUGGET Actor Andy Griffith and singer Roberta Flack were both teachers in North Carolina before becoming stars in their respective professions. Griffith taught English and drama in Goldsboro, and Flack taught music, math and English in Farmville.

DIVISION OF POWER

One State, Two State, Red State, Blue State

Since 1828, the Democratic Party has owned North Carolina. Only a handful of Republican/Whig candidates have ever carried the Tar Heel State. Between 1840 and 1964, there were only five:

☛ William Henry Harrison (Whig, 1840)

☛ Henry Clay (Whig, 1844)

☛ Zachary Taylor (Whig, 1848)

☛ Ulysses S. Grant (Rep, 1868 and 1872)

☛ Herbert Hoover (Rep, 1928)

The state changed from a blue state to a red one in 1968, voting for Richard M. Nixon in his landslide victory against George McGovern. Since that time, only two Democratic candidates (Carter in 1976 and Obama in 2008) have won North Carolina, and both went on to win the presidency.

Three U.S. presidents were born in the Tar Heel State: James K. Polk (Pineville), Andrew Johnson (Raleigh) and Andrew Jackson (Waxhaws).

Painting the Governor's Mansion Blue
North Carolina has treated the Governor's Office in a similar fashion as the White House. Since 1828, there have only been seven Republican gubernatorial winners, the last being Jim Martin, who was in office from 1985 to1993.

Overdue Perdue

In 2008, North Carolina elected its first female governor. Bev Perdue, lieutenant governor under Mike Easley, defeated Charlotte mayor Pat McCrory and claimed the big chair at the State Capitol.

North Carolina NUGGET The first governor of North Carolina was Richard Caswell. He served two terms as governor, first from 1777 to 1780, and again from 1784 to 1787. The state only allowed a maximum of three one-year terms to be served at one time during Caswell's tenure.

Districtly Speaking...

As of 2009, North Carolina has 13 congressional districts across the state, for the purposes of electing members to the U.S. House of Representatives. If you don't like politics, you probably think 13 is an unlucky number. Democrat Brad Miller, current representative of the 13th district, might disagree with you. Hopefully, people living in the district do not suffer from triskaidekaphobia.

Let's Get This Party Started

There are five officially recognized political parties in North Carolina:

☛ Constitution Party of North Carolina

☛ North Carolina Democratic Party

☛ North Carolina Green Party

☛ Libertarian Party of North Carolina

☛ North Carolina Republican Party

NOTABLE FIGURES

A True North Carolina Good 'Ole Boy

You can't talk about North Carolina politics without mentioning one of the most powerful and influential senators in history—Jesse Helms. Jesse Alexander Jr. was born in Monroe on October 18, 1921. He earned a reputation as the "farmer's senator," staunchly protecting the state's agricultural interests throughout his political tenure. Helms wasn't always a politician, though. He started his illustrious career as a sports reporter with the *Raleigh News & Observer* and went on to become executive vice president of the Capitol Broadcasting Company.

One thing is for sure, you either loved or hated Helms in North Carolina. He was one of the strongest conservative leaders this state has ever seen, and the liberals did not like his political stance. His election in 1972 was the first time since

Reconstruction that a conservative had won *any* kind of political office. Regardless of the red or blue color of your political flag, you still had to respect him for the way he protected North Carolina interests in Congress and abroad. Helms made a career of putting NC first and did so until his very last day. Helms also chaired the Senate Foreign Relations committee, one of the most powerful committees in Washington.

I worked as a governor's page in 1990 for Jim Martin and had the privilege to work in the NC Capitol. One of my jobs was to file papers, documents and other official communiqués. Several letters were from Helms, and I was able to see the senator's love for this state firsthand.

In true army veteran and political patriot fashion, Helms died on July 4, 2008.

Dewey Defeats...Helms?

One of the most talked about Senate races in North Carolina—if not United States—history involved Jesse Helms and Charlotte architect Harvey Gantt. I can remember this state being torn apart as these two politicians went head to head until the very end...literally. Several media outlets reported Gantt as the winner, including Dan Rather and CBS News. However, Helms pulled away at the last moment, and Gantt never again ran for office.

DID YOU KNOW?

West Virginia Senator Robert Byrd was born in North Wilkesboro on November 20, 1917, but not with the same name. His birth name was Cornelius Calvin Sale Jr. After his mother died while he was still an infant, he was raised by his aunt and uncle—who renamed him.

The Bigger They Are…

From pauper to prince and back, John Edwards' political career is an unfortunately familiar one in today's society. Even though he's from Robbins, South Carolina, the embattled former senator now resides in Chapel Hill. Andrew Young, the former staffer that blew the lid off Edwards' affair with Rielle Hunter, also calls Chatham County home.

Other North Carolinians Who Have Affected History

☞ **Levi Coffin (1798–1877):** Coffin was the "president" of the Underground Railroad, as well as an abolitionist and educator. (New Garden)

☞ **Hiram Revels (1827–1901):** The first African American member of the United States Congress, Revels represented Mississippi from 1870 to 1871. (Fayetteville)

☞ **O. Max Gardner (1882–1947):** Gardner was the North Carolina governor and controller of the state's Democratic "machine" between 1920 and 1940. (Shelby)

☞ **Caleb Haynes (1895–1966):** A USAF major general, Haynes is a veteran of both World Wars and the holder of 10 military awards. (Dobson)

☞ **Sam Ervin (1896–1985):** Chairman of the Watergate Commission, Ervin started the legislative ball rolling toward Nixon's resignation (Morganton).

☞ **Thad Eure (1899–1993):** Known for his bow tie and infectious smile, Eure holds the record for serving the longest term as NC's Secretary of State. (Gates County)

☞ **Terry Sanford (1917–1998):** In Sanford's multifaceted career, he was an FBI special agent, army veteran, president of Duke University, and a state senator and governor. (Laurinburg)

☞ **Robert Byrd (1917–present):** Byrd holds the distinction of being the longest-serving senator (WV) in American history. (North Wilkesboro)

☞ **Elizabeth Dole (1936–present):** Wife of Senator Bob Dole and the former Secretary of Transportation under President Reagan, Dole ran for president in 2000. (Salisbury)

☞ **Jim Hunt (1937–present):** North Carolina's longest-serving governor, Hunt served a total of four terms. He also established the North Carolina Biotechnology Center and the North Carolina School of Science and Math. (Wilson)

☞ **Erskine Bowles (1945–present):** Currently president of the University of North Carolina system, Bowles was the former White House Chief of Staff under Bill Clinton. (Greensboro)

North Carolina NUGGET To get a sneak peek through the window of the late Senator Sam Ervin's life, visit the Sam Ervin Library in his hometown of Morganton.

UNDERGROUND MOVEMENTS

Penelope's Own Tea Party

With all the Tea Party, Coffee Party and other politically motivated movements going on in the world today, some people in North Carolina do not realize that a native Tar Heel woman helped spark the resistance against British rule during the American Revolution. Edenton's Penelope Barker is considered to be America's first female political activist. Barker led a movement against British tea and cloth, much like her Boston counterparts. However, instead of dressing up a Native American and dumping tea in the Boston harbor, Barker—along with around 50 other women—wrote and signed a declaration against the British and boycotted all of the country's tea and clothing. Nary a shot was fired, but Barker's own tea party helped show the British that taxation without representation would not be tolerated by women, either.

The KKK and Governor Holden

Even though the KKK started in Pulaski, Tennessee, in 1865, during the fallout of the Civil War, North Carolina was involved with the propagation of the secret society. At the time, the Klan was not a unified organization in the state—it was more like a bunch of loosely connected bands of vigilantes, using terror and violence to influence politics, among other things. One big battle with the Klan involved Governor W.W. Holden and Union general George W. Kirk, and it was the only time martial law has ever been declared within the state's borders.

Governor Holden was having trouble controlling the Klan in Alamance and Caswell counties because the local leadership was either sympathetic to the "cause" or a part of it themselves.

The NC Legislature passed the Shoffner Act in 1870, which allowed the governor to declare any North Carolina county "to be in a state of insurrection, and to call into active service the militia of the state to such an extent as may become necessary to suppress such insurrection." Long story short, Holden sent General Kirk and a small army to Alamance and Caswell counties, and they arrested over 100 individuals suspected of Klan involvement. The "militia" ignored all the legalities and the rights of the men accused, including orders of habeas corpus from a state judge.

President U.S. Grant intervened, had all the men released and declared the counties to no longer be "in a state of insurrection." In the end, Holden was impeached from office and convicted of his crimes in 1871. Republicans in the state suffered massive defeats the next election year, and the Democrats have been in control of the state for most of the time since. Ironically, the Klan was trying to get the Democrats back in office, and Holden did it for them. Hmm...

DID YOU  KNOW?

The Greensboro Massacre of November 3, 1979, involved the Klan, the American Nazi Party and the Communist Workers' Party (CWP). Sounds like Berlin in 1943, doesn't it? The CWP (known then as the Workers' Viewpoint Organization) was trying to rally black workers into joining the organization. The marchers began heckling the Klansmen present, and later, the KKK and the Nazis began firing weapons into the crowd. Five people were killed, and several others were wounded.

The A&T/Greensboro Four

Hillary Clinton once said that "it takes a village to raise a child." Sometimes, however, it takes four students to raise awareness for a cause. Franklin McCain, Joseph McNeil, Ezell Blair Jr. and David Richmond—all NC A&T freshmen at the time—walked into the Greensboro F.W. Woolworth store on February 1, 1960. They sat down at the "whites only" lunch counter, asking to be served. They were denied service but were allowed to sit at the counter, starting the very first "sit-in." These four students kicked off hundreds of similar sit-in movements across the South, and these non-violent protests truly made a difference in the Civil Rights movement. Six months later, the Greensboro Four walked back into the same Woolworth store and were each served lunch at the very counter where the movement began.

North Carolina NUGGET On February 1, 2010, the 50th anniversary of the Greensboro Four sit-in, an archival museum and teaching facility was opened at the original spot of the first sit-in. "The International Civil Rights Center & Museum is a memorial to the courageous actions of the Greensboro Four and subsequent participants of the F.W. Woolworth sit-ins and nonviolent protests that defined a pivotal moment in the civil rights movement," said Melvin "Skip" Alston, chairman of the Museum.

PAINTERS AND SCULPTORS

What About Bob?

If you're a North Carolinian, then you've either seen or heard of Lexington's Bob Timberlake. Even if you're not a native Tar Heel, I'll bet dollars to doughnuts you've seen his work. His advancements in the realist tradition of American art are unsurpassed, and his work has been seen all over the country. His first one-man show at the Southeastern Center for Contemporary Art (SECCA) in Winston-Salem sold out before it ever opened, and his second one at Hammer Galleries in New York City did the same thing. Timberlake is, to this day, the first and only Southerner in modern history to have a one-man exhibit at the Corcoran Gallery in Washington, DC.

 Timberlake is also the official artist for the "Keep America Beautiful" and "Keep North Carolina Beautiful" campaigns. His commercials featuring Iron Eyes Cody, the Native American with a single tear running down his face, were all over TV when I was a child.

Is That Painting a Little Crooked?

The North Carolina Museum of Art (NCMA) was the first museum in the nation that was created using state funds to purchase art (139 paintings) and house it in one location. It was formed in 1947 and was probably the best $1 million ever spent. Temporarily closed for renovations, the museum reopened in April 2010 to a brand-new 127,000-square-foot expansion. There are over 160 art museums and/or art exhibits in North Carolina, including NCMA. This state sure loves its art!

North Carolina NUGGET Anna McNeill Whistler, better known as the subject of the famous oil-on-canvas masterpiece *Arrangement in Grey and Black: The Artist's Mother*, was born in Wilmington in 1804. If you think about it for a moment, you can probably figure out the name by which the painting is more famously known: *Whistler's Mother*. The painting by James McNeill Whistler is property of the French government and is currently on display at the Musée d'Orsay in Paris.

Give Him a Whirl!

Heralded as a modern-day Don Quixote, Vollis Simpson from Lucama doesn't fight windmills—he builds them! The master of the whirligig, his work has been attracting wayward travelers since he started Windmill Park in 1985. The park features

30 of his biggest creations, which are made out of materials such as machine parts, bicycle wheels and various reflectors. Simpson was even commissioned to make four whirligigs for the 1996 Summer Olympics, and they remain in downtown Atlanta to this day.

 The town of Wilson honors Simpson every year with the Wilson Whirligig Festival during the first weekend in November. The whimsical, wind-driven works of art dot the landscape around downtown Wilson, and over 20,000 people attend the festival each year.

Seeing Is Believing?

Windmill Park is also known as "Acid Park," because of an urban legend involving the death of Simpson's daughter. Rumor has it that Carol Simpson and her boyfriend were high on acid and got involved in a car accident. Carol died instantly, but the boyfriend survived and told Vollis everything he had seen. Some say that the inspiration for the park's creations came from the boyfriend's description of what he saw while under the influence. A multitude of reflectors adorn the structures, creating an eerie glow when viewed at night.

DID YOU KNOW?

North Carolina painter Herb Jackson—whose work is in more than 80 collections, including the British Museum in London, England, and the Brooklyn Museum in New York City—was presented with the North Carolina Award in 1999 by then-governor Jim Hunt. The award is the highest civilian honor that can be bestowed in the state.

Big Art

The *Guinness Book of Records 2003* holder for the world's largest painting on canvas by one artist was unveiled in North

Carolina. In 2001, Canadian artist Eric Waugh created *Hero*, a 41,400-square-foot masterpiece and debuted it at North Carolina's Museum of Art in Raleigh. The massive painting was a fundraising and public awareness campaign initiated by Waugh to help enhance the lives of children suffering from HIV and AIDS, as well as to raise money for Camp Heartland in Minneapolis, Minnesota.

Red Clay Ramblin'

Clay covers a big portion of North Carolina, and one area of the state has found a pretty good use for it. The town of Seagrove is smack dab in the middle of one of the state's key historical pottery-producing regions. It is also home to the North Carolina Pottery Center, which showcases the state's artistic history and rich clay heritage. There's even a Seagrove Area Potters' Association (SAPA), of which potters like Mark and Meredith Heywood—representing Whynot Pottery—are members. All the potters are listed alphabetically, or you could even pick a random potter. Would Harry do?

MUSIC AND ENTERTAINMENT

Idol Worship

FOX's *American Idol* should set up a permanent scouting location in North Carolina because several contestants have been from the Tar Heel State:

- Clay Aiken (Raleigh, Season 2 runner-up)

- Fantasia Barrino (High Point, Season 3 winner)

- Charly Lowry (Pembroke, Season 3)

- Sarah Mather (Wilmington, Season 4)

- Bucky Covington (Rockingham, Season 5)

- Heather Cox (Jonesville, Season 5)

- Chris Daughtry (McLeansville, Season 5)

- Kelly Pickler (Albemarle, Season 5)

- Anoop Desai (Chapel Hill, Season 8)

 Rock and Roll Hall of Fame inductee George Clinton, a member of Parliament and Funkadelic, was born in Kannapolis on July 22, 1941.

What It Was, Was Football...

Andy Griffith recorded this cult classic stand-up comedy routine in 1953, and friends, listenin' to it made me fit to be tied with laughter. Yes, it did. (You have to hear the football skit to understand.)

Born in Mt. Airy, Griffith overcame a poor childhood to graduate from UNC-Chapel Hill and become a part of the

oldest national fraternity for men in music—the Phi Mu Alpha Sinfonia. A short time later, he was casted in *The Lost Colony* play in Manteo and broke it big with his dramatic role in the film *A Face in the Crowd* (1957). However, the role that would change his life—along with most of America—came in 1960, when he was cast as Sheriff Andy Taylor in the *Andy Griffith Show*. The show instantly became a hit, and Griffith became one of North Carolina's most beloved celebrities. The show was ranked ninth on *TV Guide*'s list of the 50 Greatest TV Shows of All Time in 2002.

A statue of Sheriff Taylor and his son, Opie (played by film director Ron Howard), as they were going fishing in the opening credits of the show, can be found in his hometown of Mt. Airy. A similar version of the *Goin' Fishin'* statue can be found at Raleigh's Pullen Park. I can hear the whistlin' now…

DID YOU  KNOW?

Griffith is also a Grammy Award–winning southern gospel singer. Yes, he is.

Hollywood East

Who says all movies are filmed in Hollywood? Not so! As of 2008, Wilmington is ranked third in movie production in the U.S., and the city's film industry continues to grow in leaps and bounds. Famed director Dino De Laurentiis started a film production company in the booming coastal town in the 1970s, and Wilmington has never looked back. Films, television shows, commercials—all wrapped up in the Hollywood of the South.

DID YOU  KNOW?

D.W. Griffith based the first epic in movie history, *The Birth of a Nation* (1915), on the novel *The Clansman*, by Shelby native Thomas F. Dixon Jr.

And That's a Wrap

According to the North Carolina Film Office, there are six full-service film studios in operation across the state: Carolina Pinnacle (Greensboro), Creative Networks (Charlotte), EUE/Screen Gems (Wilmington), Earl Owensby Studios (Charlotte), Silver Hammer (Charlotte) and Trailblazer (Raleigh).

From Grabtown Girl to Tinseltown Legend

Born in Brogden (just east of Smithfield), stunningly beautiful actress Ava Gardner was a Johnston County girl through and through. As my neighbors say now, JoCo Girls are the best in the world. Because of her local ties, the town of Smithfield created the Ava Gardner Museum downtown so that fans of the Johnston County celebrity could have a permanent place to enjoy her beauty and her life's accomplishments.

DID YOU KNOW?

Ava Gardner is buried in Sunset Memorial Park at the corner of Highways 70 and 301 in Smithfield, and the first radio station I ever worked at—1090 AM WBZB—was located along a service road in that very cemetery. Cool!

North Carolina NUGGET Actress Jada Pinkett Smith, wife of megastar Will Smith, attended the North Carolina School of the Arts in Winston-Salem for a short time and majored in theater.

Some Films Shot Partially or Completely in North Carolina

Leatherheads (2008)
Nights in Rodanthe (2008)
The Secret Life of Bees (2008)
The Guardian (2006)
Talladega Nights: The Ballad of Ricky Bobby (2006)
3: The Dale Earnhardt Story (2004)
Juwanna Mann (2002)
A Walk to Remember (2002)
Cabin Fever (2002)
Divine Secrets of the Ya-Ya Sisterhood (2002)
Domestic Disturbance (2001)
Hannibal (2001)
Shallow Hal (2001)
Summer Catch (2001)
28 Days (2000)
Weekend at Bernie's (1989)
The Green Mile (1999)
He Got Game (1998)
Patch Adams (1998)
I Know What You Did Last Summer (1997)
Lolita (1997)
The Jackal (1997)

Kiss the Girls (1997)
The Crow (1994)
Forrest Gump (1994)
The Hudsucker Proxy (1994)
The Road to Wellville (1994)
Amos and Andrew (1993)
The Fugitive (1993)
The Program (1993)
Super Mario Brothers (1993)
The Last of the Mohicans (1992)
Billy Bathgate (1991)
Sleeping with the Enemy (1991)
Days of Thunder (1990)
The Hunt for Red October (1990)
Mr. Destiny (1990)
Teenage Mutant Ninja Turtles (1990)
Bull Durham (1988)
Dirty Dancing (1987)
Blue Velvet (1986)
Manhunter (1986)
The Color Purple (1985)
Firestarter (1984)
Stroker Ace (1983)
Deliverance (1972)

TV, RADIO AND PRINT

On the Road with Charles

Charles Kuralt was one of journalism's true pioneers and legends, and he was happy to call North Carolina home. Born in Wilmington, Kuralt grew up loving the Tar Heel state and wanted to share his love of travel with others. He attended UNC-Chapel Hill and was the editor of the college newspaper, *The Daily Tar Heel*. Soon after, he was hired by CBS and worked his way up to the *Evening News with Walter Cronkite*. His famous "On the Road" segments started there in 1967 and continued until 1980. I can still remember waking up to his dulcet tones on *CBS Sunday Morning*, a job he took after ending the "On the Road" series. He anchored the Sunday morning program until he retired in 1994. He stayed in journalism, traveling the country in 1994 and 1995, searching for material for a new book, *Charles Kuralt's America*.

DID YOU **KNOW?**

In 1977, Kuralt added the text to a book by artist Bob Timberlake entitled *The Bob Timberlake Collection*.

 Two of the world's most famous journalists of all time—Edward R. Murrow (near Greensboro) and David Brinkley (Wilmington)—were born in North Carolina.

Moonlighting

WRAL News anchors Bill Leslie and Pam Saulsby have made quite a name for themselves in the music industry. Leslie, a member of the band Lorica, and Saulsby, a soulful jazz vocalist, can both be found singing and playing all around the

Triangle when they're not working at the state's most recognizable television news station.

Loud and Clear

The first musical notes ever sent across radio waves happened in the Tar Heel State in 1902. R.A. Fessenden performed those sound tests in Buxton, and the broadcast was received 48 miles away near Roanoke Island. Were cans and string involved? I'm not sure…

DID YOU KNOW?

Musician John Tesh came through the Old North State, graduating from North Carolina State University in 1975. He also worked as a television anchor at WTVD in Durham.

Quoth the Raven, "Here Are Two More…"
Emily Mallory Proctor, who plays criminologist Calleigh Duquesne on *CSI: Miami*, was born in Raleigh in 1968. She attended Ravenscroft School ('86) in Raleigh and graduated from East Carolina University in Greenville. Proctor got her break into television as a weather anchor at WNCT-TV in Greenville. Another Ravenscroft graduate ('89) is finding a name for himself on television. Michael C. Hall, known for the lead role on the Showtime drama *Dexter*, was born in Raleigh in 1971.

North Carolina NUGGET Political legend and conservative firebrand Jesse Helms worked in radio before hitting the political trail. He was actually the news and program director at 101.5 WRAL-FM from 1948 to 1951.

All the News That's Fit to Print

North Carolina's first newspaper was the *North Carolina Gazette*, which started operation in 1751. Over 2000 newspapers have been published in the Tar Heel state since the *Gazette* first appeared in New Bern. Some of the biggest papers in the state—the *Raleigh News & Observer*, *Charlotte Observer*, *Winston-Salem Journal* and *Greensboro News & Record*—have been around a long time and continue to crank out news on a daily basis.

North Carolina NUGGET Recognized as the world's smallest daily newspaper, the *Tryon Daily Bulletin*, which started in 1928, was once about the size of a *Reader's Digest* magazine. It was enlarged to regular printer-paper size (8.5" x 11") in 1955.

LITERATURE

A Wolfe in Writer's Clothing

One of the most prolific writers of his day, Thomas Wolfe is one of Asheville's most famous people. Author of *Look Homeward, Angel* and *You Can't Go Home Again*, as well as several short stories, poems and screenplays, Wolfe focused on the changing of America and the illusions of prosperity. He created some serious tension with *Angel* because it was a semi-autobiographical novel about his time growing up in Asheville. He changed the name of the town to Altamont and the place where he grew up to Dixieland, and he even gave his character a new name—Eugene Gant. He had to stay away from Asheville for eight years after the book was published because the townspeople weren't too happy with some of their portrayals. Ironically, when his next book, *The October Fair*, came out, people in Asheville were once again displeased because they *weren't* mentioned.

 The first novel about North Carolina, *Eoneguski, or Cherokee Chief*, was written by U.S. Senator Robert Strange in 1839.

With a Twist

William Sydney Porter was born near Greensboro on September 11, 1862, and moved to Texas when he was 20 years old. He ran into some legal trouble and was arrested and convicted for embezzlement. While serving his five-year prison sentence, Porter came up with the pen name O. Henry and began his storied literary career. Can I call that a twist beginning?

Being Greensboro's native son, O. Henry has had two hotels in the city named after him. The original O. Henry Hotel was built in downtown Greensboro in 1919 and demolished in 1979. Proprietors Dennis and Nancy King Quaintance opened the new O. Henry Hotel in 1998.

DID YOU  **KNOW?**

O. Henry was the first man to coin the phrase "banana republic" in his short story *Cabbages and Kings*. He wrote the tale while hiding out from the police in Honduras in 1896. It wasn't published until 1904.

 O. Henry and Thomas Wolfe are buried in the same Asheville resting place— Riverside Cemetery. Some other famous North Carolinians are buried there as well, including NC's Civil War governor, Zebulon B. Vance.

Oh, Bugger…
Ender's Game by Greensboro author Orson Scott Card is a science-fiction tour de force. It won the Nebula Award (1985) and the Hugo Award (1986), considered the two biggest science-fiction writing awards. Card created an entire world around main character Andrew "Ender" Wiggin, and a movie version of *Ender's Game* is also in the works. I also teach this book in my high school English class. Weird, I know.

DID YOU  KNOW?

Nicholas Sparks, author of *The Notebook* and *Dear John*, calls New Bern home. He also coached New Bern High School's track team, focusing on the 400-meter and 800-meter events. Sparks was a collegiate track star with the University of Notre Dame.

How Can a Name...Break Your Heart?

Wounded Confederate deserter W.P. Inman spoke these words in the National Book Award–winning novel *Cold Mountain*, written by Asheville's Charles Frazier. Frazier's novel beautifully captures the culture and the way of life of the North Carolina mountains during the Civil War and was based on the stories surrounding his own great-uncle. After experiencing great success with his debut novel, it was turned into a major motion picture starring Jude Law, Nicole Kidman and Renée Zellweger. Frazier now raises horses on a farm near Raleigh.

DID YOU  KNOW?

The Disney movie classic *Escape to Witch Mountain* was originally a novel written by Franklin author Alexander Key in 1968.

An American First

Thomas Harriot is credited with writing the first book published by an English colonist in America in 1588. The manuscript, *A Briefe and True Report of the New Found Land of Virginia*, is still considered the cornerstone of North American natural history. It was written while Harriot was an explorer for Sir Walter Raleigh near Roanoke.

North Carolina NUGGET Noted *Great Gatsby* author F. Scott Fitzgerald was once believed to have committed suicide at the Grove Park Inn in Asheville. Fitzgerald was living at the inn while his wife, Zelda, was a patient at the Highland Mental Hospital. In the summer of 1936, Fitzgerald—worried about debts, lack of income and his ailing wife—fired a revolver as a threat of suicide, and the inn refused to let him stay alone after that. A portrait of Fitzgerald still hangs in the Grove Park Inn to this day.

No Bones About It
Famed author and forensic anthropologist Kathy Reichs, known for her Temperance Brennan novel series, is a professor at the University of North Carolina at Charlotte. The series has been adapted (albeit loosely) into the FOX television show *Bones*, starring Emily Deschanel and David Boreanaz. What's cool about the series is that Brennan's character in the show is an author as well. The name of her female protagonist? Kathy Reichs. Quid pro quo.

DID YOU KNOW?

Poet Maya Angelou, author of *I Know Why the Caged Bird Sings* and Clinton's inaugural poem "On the Pulse of the Morning," is also the Reynolds Professor of American Studies at Wake Forest University in Winston-Salem. The university also opened a new facility named after her—the Maya Angelou Center for Health Equity.

Black Bard

Slave poet George Moses Horton published the first book by a black author in the South, *The Hope of Liberty*, in 1829. Horton called himself "the colored bard of North Carolina."

ARCHITECTURE AND DESIGN

Not Just Your Average Catholic Church

The Minor Basilica of St. Lawrence is a majestic structure located in Asheville. It was built in 1909 by Spanish architect Rafael Guastavino. Guastavino helped develop and improve the "tile arch" architectural system, which is now called the "Guastavino" tile system. This basilica has the largest free-standing elliptical dome in the country and is considered to be the Mother Church of western North Carolina. The Spanish architect also helped design the largest private residence in the nation, the Biltmore Estate. Guastavino's final resting place is inside his impressive basilica.

DID YOU  **KNOW?**

The architect of the Lincoln Memorial, Henry Bacon Jr., lived in Southport and Wilmington from 1876 to 1924.

The Elliptical Wonder

Some people refer to the J.S. Dorton Arena on the North Carolina State Fairgrounds as the Cow Palace. The architect, Matthew Nowicki, called it the Paraboleum. The concave building, constructed in 1952, is one of the most recognizable structures in the entire state. I can remember driving past Dorton Arena as child, right along Hillsborough Street, and asking my father why the roof had fallen in on the round building. He just laughed and kept on driving. I've seen hockey games (Raleigh Icecaps), professional wrestling matches, concerts, roller derby matches (Carolina Rollergirls) and many other events in Dorton Arena. It is definitely one of the most original buildings you'll ever see.

North Carolina NUGGET The North Carolina Governor's Mansion was designed by two Philadelphia architects but was built using mainly prison labor from inmates at Central Prison in Raleigh. The prison warden, William J. Hicks, is credited with overseeing the mansion's construction.

Duke Chapel

Without a doubt, the Duke University Chapel is one of the most breathtaking works of architecture I have ever seen. Built in the English gothic style between 1930 and 1932, the chapel stands over 210 feet high and seats close to 2000 people. The tower was modeled by a Philadelphia architectural firm after Canterbury Cathedral and is one of the tallest structures in

Durham County. The chapel also has three pipe organs, with close to 13,000 pipes in total! Former governor and longtime Duke president Terry Sanford is buried beneath the chapel, along with Buck Duke's wife, Nanaline Holt Duke, and several other dignitaries.

DID YOU KNOW?

The Newbold-White House in Hertford, built in 1730, is the oldest brick house in the state.

North Carolina NUGGET Robert R. Taylor, the pioneering black architect who designed 10 of the buildings at Booker T. Washington's Tuskegee Institute, was born in Wilmington in 1868.

BIRTHPLACE: NORTH CAROLINA

Okay, there are way too many famous North Carolinians to fit into this section, so I will try my best to hit the high points.

NC Entertainers

Look very closely, and you might see a name or three you recognize. If not, then you've been under a rock for the last few years. The Tar Heel State has produced some seriously heavy hitters in the arts-and-entertainment field—in many different genres.

- ☞ Sandra Bullock, actress (graduated from East Carolina University in Greenville)

- ☞ Rick Dees, host of radio's *Weekly Top 40* (Greensboro)

- ☞ Cecil B. DeMille, film director (Washington)

- ☞ Zack Galifianakis, comedian (Sparta)

- ☞ Gallagher, comedian/watermelon destroyer (Ft. Bragg)

- ☞ Billy Graham, the most famous evangelical preacher in the world (Montreat)

- ☞ Pam Grier, actress (Winston-Salem)

- ☞ Jeff Hardy, wrestler (Cameron)

- ☞ Matt Hardy, wrestler (Cameron)

- ☞ Rebekah Revels Lowry, former Miss North Carolina (Pembroke)

- ☞ Vince McMahon, president of World Wrestling Entertainment (Pinehurst)

- ☞ Julianne Moore, actress (Fayetteville)

- ☞ Mary-Louise Parker, actress (graduated from NCSA in Winston-Salem)

- ☞ Jaime Pressly, actress/model (Kinston)

- ☞ Soupy Sales, comedian (Franklinton)

- ☞ Gregory Shane "The Hurricane" Helms, wrestler (Smithfield)

- ☞ Reginald VelJohnson, actor (Raleigh)

- ☞ Ben Vereen, actor (Laurinburg)

- ☞ Evan Rachel Wood, actress (Raleigh)

NC Musicians

Growing up in North Carolina, I was able to hear every musical genre possible—from southern gospel and country at my grandmother's house to rock and hip-hop in the speakers of my 1977 Buick Regal land yacht. From bluegrass to rap, from beach to alternative, from jazz to everything else in between, the state has it all.

☛ Tori Amos, singer (Newton)

☛ Shirley Caesar, singer (Durham)

- John Coltrane, jazz musician (Hamlet)

- The Connells, alternative band (Raleigh)

- Charlie Daniels, singer/songwriter (Wilmington)

- Jermaine Dupri, rap artist and record producer (Asheville)

- Fred Durst, frontman for Limp Bizkit (Gastonia)

- The Embers, beach musicians (Raleigh)

- Donna Fargo, singer/songwriter (Mt. Airy)

- Roberta Flack, singer (Asheville)

- Ben Folds, singer/songwriter (Winston-Salem/Chapel Hill)

- Randy Jones, singer of the Village People (Raleigh)

- Ben E. King, singer/songwriter (Henderson)

- Ronnie Milsap, country singer (Robbinsville)

- Theolonious Monk, jazz pianist/composer (Rocky Mount)

- Petey Pablo, rap artist (Greenville)

- Max Roach, jazz drummer (Pasquotank County)

- Earl Scruggs, bluegrass banjo player (Shelby)

- Nina Simone, singer (Tryon)

- Squirrel Nut Zippers, musicians (Chapel Hill/Efland)

- Randy Travis, country music singer (Marshville)

- Doc Watson, folk guitarist (Deep Gap)

- Jimmy Wayne, country singer (Kings Mountain)

NC Authors

As an author and English teacher, many of these names are familiar to me. Hopefully, they'll all become familiar to you as well. There are some prolific literary names here—and many more than I could list.

- ☛ Lillian Jackson Braun (Tryon)

- ☛ Jerry Bledsoe (Asheboro)

- ☛ Fred Chappell (Canton)

- ☛ Patricia Cornwell (Montreat)

- ☛ Sarah Dessen (Chapel Hill)

- ☛ Pamela Duncan (Asheville)

- ☛ Clyde Edgerton (Durham)

- ☛ Kaye Gibbons (Nash County)

- ☛ Allan Gurganus (Rocky Mount)

- ☛ Mur Lafferty (Durham)

- ☛ Margaret Maron (Greensboro)

- ☛ Jill McCorkle (Lumberton)

- ☛ Robert Morgan (Hendersonville)

- ☛ Reynolds Price (Macon)

- ☛ David Sedaris (spent his childhood in Raleigh)

- ☛ Timothy Tyson (Oxford)

- ☛ Donald Vaughan (Raleigh)

BLINDED ME WITH SCIENCE

Build It and They Will Research

What happens when you get the best and brightest scientists, pharmacists and other researchers together in one place? Progress, change, innovation…otherwise known as Research Triangle Park (RTP). RTP, a model for research, innovation and economic development, was founded in January 1959 by a committee of government, university and business leaders. Their hope was to improve the economic framework of the state, therefore giving North Carolinians better opportunities to succeed. Two of RTP's most significant discoveries are Taxol, the most important anti-cancer drug for the past 15 years (according to the National Cancer Institute) and the successful HIV-AIDS drug AZT. Some of RTP's largest employers include IBM Corporation, GlaxoSmithKline, Cisco, Nortel, RTI International, Fidelity Investments, the U.S. Environmental Protection Agency (EPA), the National Institute of Environmental Health Sciences, NetApp, Biogen IDEC and Sony Ericsson. RTP has over 42,000 people working there, with a combined annual payroll of almost $2.7 billion. The average individual salary in RTO is 45 percent larger than the regional and national average—sitting firmly at $56,000 annually.

DID YOU  **KNOW?**

RTP's EPA building is one of the largest "green" buildings in the world (Merchandise Mart, located in Chicago, is the largest), and the NCEPA campus is the largest in the agency.

 Established in October 1984, the North Carolina Biotechnology Center was the world's first government-sponsored biotechnology center. Since its founding, the center has invested around $200 million into the infrastructure of the state's biotechnology network. According to professional services firm Ernst & Young, North Carolina is now the nation's third-leading state for biotechnology—with almost 530 bioscience companies employing nearly 58,000 people.

Primary Primates

Established in 1966, the Duke University Lemur Center (DLC) is the world's largest sanctuary for rare and endangered prosimian primates. A prosimian is a primate that is not a monkey, ape or human. Housed on 85 acres of the Durham campus, over 250 animals call the center home—including

233 lemurs (over 15 species), Indian and Southeast Asian lorises and African bushbabies. The DLC is located on Lemur Lane in Durham.

DID YOU KNOW?

The 2001 Emmy Award–winning PBS show *Zoboomafoo* was filmed on location at the DLC. Zoboo's real name was Jovian, and he was a Coquerel's sifaka that was born at the DLC in 1994.

Bring Me a Shrubbery!

Dr. J.C. Raulston revolutionized the United States nursery industry through his work in North Carolina. Working with NC State University, Raulston was the director of the NC State Arboretum, an eight-acre masterpiece located in Raleigh and maintained largely by NCSU faculty, students and volunteers. Plant collections include over 5000 total species and/or cultivars of annuals, perennials, bulbs, vines, groundcovers, shrubs and trees from over 50 different countries. The arboretum also has the most diverse collection of cold-hardy temperate zone plants in the southeastern United States. Dr. Raulston promoted plants such as the Leyland cypress, the "Little Gem" magnolia and the Japanese cedar. Dr. Richard Lighty, the first director of the Mount Cuba Center in Delaware, once cited Dr. Raulston as "having put more plants into the hands of those who could get them into production than anyone else in America." The NC State Arboretum has since been renamed the J.C. Raulston Arboretum.

DID YOU KNOW?

The symbol of the arboretum is the red lace-leaf Japanese maple (*Acer palmatum* Dissectum Atropurpureum Group), a tree that has long been connected with Dr. Raulston.

 Raleigh author Bobby J. Ward wrote a book about Dr. Raulston's life entitled *Chlorophyll in his Veins.* Clever title…it kinda grows on you.

It's *Not* Dirt

My wife, a middle school science teacher, corrects me just about every time I say the word "dirt." "It's not dirt, honey. It's soil," she says. Another North Carolinian that would correct me would be Hugh Bennett, considered to be the "Father of Soil Conservation." Born in 1881 near Wadesboro, Bennett went on to be the first chief of the Soil Conservation Service, a branch of the U.S. Department of Agriculture, from 1935 to 1952. Bennett helped to establish the Brown Creek Soil Conservation District in 1937, the first district in America concerned with erosion control. Ironically, Brown Creek includes Bennett's plantation birthplace.

INVENTIONS, DISCOVERIES AND BREAKTHROUGHS

The Taste of the Carolinas

Born in Chinquapin, pharmacist Caleb Bradham returned to the Tar Heel State in the early 1890s after graduating from the University of Maryland's School of Medicine. He opened a drugstore in New Bern and had a soda fountain installed. One of the draws to the Bradham Drug Company in 1893 was "Brad's Drink," an invention featuring a blend of carbonated water, sugar, pepsin, kola nut extract, vanilla and other "rare oils." Bradham touted the drink as an aid to digestion because of the pepsin additive. The properties and popularity of Brad's Drink led Bradham to rename his invention "Pepsi-Cola" in 1898—paying homage to the pepsin and kola nut ingredients. On December 24, 1902, the Pepsi-Cola Company was incorporated in the state of North Carolina.

DID YOU KNOW?

The Coca-Cola Bottling Company was offered a chance to buy Pepsi-Cola on three separate occasions between 1922 and 1933 and declined all three. Oops.

Cheerwine, a "cherry different soft drink" that popped its first top in Salisbury in 1917, was not trademarked until 1926. The question you always hear from people unfamiliar with the drink is, "Is it really a wine?" The cherry-flavored soft drink is no more alcoholic than root beer. The founder, L.D. Peeler, thought the drink had the deep red color of wine and had "happy" bubbles—thus, Cheerwine was born.

The "Hot" Sign Is On!

Vernon Rudolph and two other men drove from Nashville, Tennessee, to Winston-Salem in 1937 with $25, some baking equipment and the elusive secret recipe for Krispy Kreme doughnuts (a handwritten recipe scribbled on a piece of paper). They rented retail space in what is now called historic Old Salem, across from Salem College, then set up shop and began to develop their business. On July 13, 1937, the first Krispy Kreme doughnuts were made. Since then, the "Hot" sign has been on for millions of Americans, and Krispy Kreme opened their first store outside the United States in Mississauga, Ontario, Canada, on December 11, 2001. There's nothing better than a warm, glazed Krispy Kreme doughnut right off of the conveyor belt. Sugary heaven!

A Funny Thing Happened on the Way to San Juan...

On my honeymoon in 2004, my new wife and I were traveling
from Raleigh to Seattle, Washington, for a week's vacation in
the San Juan Islands. We landed in Seattle around 1:00 AM
and began our midnight drive to Anacortes to catch our ferry.
My wife is a serious coffee drinker and wanted an authentic
cup of Seattle's historic coffee. We drove around for what
seemed like forever, and what was the only store we found
open at 1:00 AM? A Krispy Kreme doughnut shop just north
of Seattle—3000 miles away and we had a little piece of home
waiting for us.

Having a Ball...Bucky Style!

Buckminster Fuller was called "a 20th-century Da Vinci,
a modern Ben Franklin and a jet-age Emerson." An architect,
designer, poet and visionary, Fuller is best known for the creation of the geodesic dome in the 1940s, which he thought

would help alleviate the pressing housing problem faced by the United States after World War II.

Geodesic literally means "earth dividing." Fuller took a sphere and divided it into equal triangles—each surface of the triangle allowing the stress to be distributed evenly across its surface. His first dome was constructed while he was teaching at Black Mountain College in western North Carolina. He also created the Dymaxion car, whose name is derived from "dynamic" and "maximum efficiency."

In February 1896, Henry Louis Smith, physics professor and later president at Davidson College, was the first professional in North Carolina to perfect the medical application of X-rays.

That Stuff's Made in…Winston-Salem?

With a name like Texas Pete, most people automatically think the hot sauce was developed and bottled in the Lone Star State. However, the spicy additive was created by Thad Garner, owner of the Dixie Pig barbecue stand in Winston-Salem, in 1929.

Where'd the name come from? Well, the story is told that the Garner family was kicking around a few names and "Mexican Joe" came up. Thad's father, Samuel, felt the name should be more American sounding. They came up with the state of Texas, known for its spicy culture and combined it with the nickname of Thad's brother Harold. "Texas Pete" is now immortalized on every bottle emblazoned with the silhouetted cowboy.

Rat-a-Tat-Tat!

The first rapid-fire machine gun shot onto the scene in 1861, thanks to North Carolina native Richard J. Gatling.

North Carolina NUGGET Greensboro pharmacist Lunsford Richardson created Vick's Croup and Pneumonia Salve (now Vick's VapoRub) in 1891. The Vick's name honors Richardson's brother-in-law, Dr. Joshua Vick.

LONG ARM OF THE LAW

How Dangerous Is North Carolina?

According to the Federal Bureau of Investigation, North Carolina's overall crime rate in 2008 was 4554.6 crimes per 100,000 residents, down from just over 4600 in 2007. Now, when you split the rates between violent (rape, murder, robbery and aggravated assault) and property (burglary, larceny and vehicle theft) crimes, the story is a little different. The violent crime rate is right along with the national rate, while the property crime rate has been trending above the national rate since 1992.

Enjoy Your Summer!

The summer months of July and August tend to be the biggest violent crime months in North Carolina, but only slightly. However, they're also some of the most beautiful months here as well.

North Carolina NUGGET The county with the highest violent crime rate in 2008 was Robeson (946.0 per 100,000 residents). The lowest violent crime rate that same year was in Madison County (21.1). The highest property crime rate was Vance County (7427.2), and the lowest was found in Alleghany County (496.0).

Stealing Home

By far and away, larceny/theft is the most common crime in North Carolina. In 2008, 228,259 arrests were made, with a rate of 2561.6 crimes per 100,000 residents. On the plus side, at least it came down from 2007 (2632.1). The national rate was 2167.0 in 2008. Compared with Arizona (2849.5), South Carolina (2814.1) and Tennessee (2687.3), the numbers don't look quite so bad.

Edward Stickyhands

Maybe Winona Ryder has had more influence on North Carolina than she realizes. Shoplifting arrests were up 17 percent in 2008, with a total of 33,322 arrests across the state.

Change for the Better

In 2008, larceny/theft from coin machines dropped 32 percent from 2007. Now that's change you can count on.

Not Quite as Aggravating

Even though the state's aggravated assault rate in 2008 (284.3 crimes per 100,000 residents) is above the national rate (274.6), it has come down tremendously since 1999—by almost 100 points. Back then, it was an aggravating 354.4.

Don't Drink and Drive

The North Carolina Highway Patrol and other law enforce-ment agencies are always on the lookout for impaired drivers. It seems like they found their fair share between 2007 and 2008. In those two years, police arrested 1284 drivers under the age of 18 and 106,792 adult drivers. Yikes!

LOCAL LAWS OF INTEREST

The Key to Success

You may think you sound like James Taylor or Shirley Caesar, but if you sing off-key for longer than 90 seconds in Nags Head, they'll nag you with a fine.

Look, Ma...No Hands!

Although doing bicycle tricks may be fun, it will land you with a hefty fine if you're caught in Kill Devil Hills. The law there says that no person shall ride a bicycle through town without both hands on the handlebars.

I Saw That Coming...

If you did, then you might be guilty of a crime. No one can practice palmistry or fortune-telling as a professional in North Carolina. If you are in a school or a church setting, however, you can do it as an amateur.

Plowing the Fields

North Carolina has long been known for its textile and agricultural prowess. However, Dumbo cannot help you plow your fields. In North Carolina, it is illegal to use an elephant to harvest a cotton field. Aww, peanuts.

Whoa There, Buddy...

If you're driving to the town of Forest City, you have to pull over to the side of the road before entering city limits. By law, you have to call Town Hall and tell them a car is coming into town. The reason? The people on Main Street need time to secure their horses so that the engine won't spook them.

Put 'Em Up, Put 'Em Up…

Canines and felines haven't been getting along for centuries—just ask Tom the cat and every dog that helped protect Jerry the mouse. Tom would be safe in the town of Barber, however, because a local statute makes fights between dogs and cats illegal. Sorry, Jerry.

Enjoy Your Stay…er, Marriage

Something always told me not to lie on hotel registration forms. Why, you ask? Well, if an unmarried couple (man and woman) check into a hotel and they check the "married" box on the registration form, then by the power vested by the state of North Carolina, they are officially husband and wife. Check out time is 11:00 AM.

Dry Bingo

No need to worry about Grandma tying one on at the local bingo parlor. According to state law, serving alcohol at a bingo game or at any other house of entertainment is a big no-no.

Other Crazy Crimes

☛ It is illegal to have sex in a churchyard.

☛ It is against the law to play a piccolo in Tryon between the hours of 11:00 PM and 7:30 AM.

☛ It is illegal for children under the age of seven to go to college in Winston-Salem.

☛ All couples staying overnight in a hotel must have a room with double beds that are at least two feet apart. Making love in the space between the beds is strictly forbidden.

☛ In Asheville, it's illegal to sneeze on city streets.

☛ In Rocky Mount, a person must pay property taxes on their canine companion.

☛ It is illegal to have sex in any position other than missionary.

MOST DANGEROUS PLACES

You're Safe with Me

According to research compiled by CQ Press, publisher of *America's Safest (And Most Dangerous Cities)*, the top five safest metropolitan North Carolina cities in 2009 were as follows:

☛ Cary (ranked 19th safest nationally)

☛ Jacksonville (150th)

☛ Raleigh (199th)

☛ Greenville (267th)

☛ High Point (286th)

By the same token, the top five least-safe metropolitan cities were:

☛ Fayetteville (340th safest)

☛ Charlotte (324th)

☛ Winston-Salem (320th)

☛ Greensboro (319th)

☛ Wilmington (307th)

"Cary" On, My Wayward Son

North Carolina's safest city has a history of manicured sidewalks, strict neighborhood and business owners associations and rapidly growing populations. Between 2007 and 2008, Raleigh/Cary was the nation's fastest-growing metropolitan area according to the U.S. Census Bureau. That does explain the traffic headaches along the U.S. 1 corridor. In 2008, Cary had 107 violent crimes and 2340 property crimes reported, compared to Fayetteville's numbers—1614 violent crimes and 13,505 property crimes reported.

North Carolina NUGGET Locals think that Cary's town name is an acronym that stands for "Consolidated Area of Relocated Yankees." When I lived in an apartment there in 1995, six of the seven people who lived in the same unit as I did were from New York. Coinkydink?

Not the "Ville"-an

Fayetteville may be ranked as North Carolina's most dangerous city, but those numbers may be a little misleading. Yes, the violent crime rate is 87 percent higher than the national average. Yes, the property crime rate is 75 percent higher. However, the 2008 rate is the lowest that Fayetteville has seen since 2000. They must be doing something right.

Where's the Bull City?

For years, Durham has had the reputation for being a city on the wrong side of secure. Although it has unsafe areas, the Bull City was only ranked as the sixth least-safe city in North Carolina, according to CQ Press. Having worked there for WDNC radio, it is a pretty great city.

Danger, Will Robinson…If You're on Foot

Have you ever heard of the Pedestrian Danger Index (PDI)? Well, the Transportation 4 America folks define it as a measure of the relative risk of walking, adjusted for exposure, and it is calculated by dividing the average pedestrian fatality rate by the percentage of residents walking to work. Based on numbers from the year 2000, the town with the highest PDI was Rocky Mount, with a score of 201.8, compared to the town with the nation's highest PDI—Macon, Georgia (398.9). The safest town to take a stroll in is Jacksonville, with a score of 32.2.

(IN)FAMOUS CRIMINALS

Avast, Me Hearties!

There has never been another criminal in the history of North Carolina more famous or more feared than Blackbeard the pirate. The diabolical scavenger of the sea trolled around the East Coast in the early 18th century, preferring to stay near the North Carolina town of Ocracoke. The stories are abundant surrounding the famous pirate, whose real name is believed to have been either Edward Teach or Edward Thatch. One of my favorite things about this notorious pirate was that he put long-burning cannon fuses into his beard, which created mysterious wisps of smoke around his head. The most fearsome pirate ever to sail the scurvy seas, Blackbeard's reputation alone forced captains to give up their ships and cargo without a fight. Once his pirate flag was visible, seafarers knew their fate was sealed.

Blackbeard's reign of terror came to an end shortly after Virginia governor Alexander Spotswood let loose the hounds. He heard that Blackbeard and his crew had received a North Carolina governor's pardon from Charles Eden, but the rogue continued to plunder areas near Bath and Ocracoke Inlet. Spotswood sent the Royal Navy, along with Captain Robert Maynard, to apprehend the nefarious pirate. And apprehend they did—on November 22, 1718, Blackbeard was shot five times, stabbed more than 20 times and decapitated. Maynard took Blackbeard's head and placed it on the bowsprit of his ship, which was how he planned to prove that he had killed the pirate so he could collect his reward from Spotswood.

Because of the fear the pirate had instilled in his men and other men of the sea, stories surrounding Blackbeard's death appeared almost immediately. Locals in the area still say that when his headless body was tossed overboard, it swam three times around the pirate's own ship before sinking below the surface. To quote Count Floyd from *SCTV*, "Ooooh, scary!"

 Blackbeard's flagship, the *Queen Anne's Revenge*, was originally the British vessel *Concord*. The French captured it and renamed her *La Concorde de Nantes*. Pirates captured the vessel again and dubbed her the *Queen Anne's Revenge*. Blackbeard ran the vessel aground in Beaufort Inlet in June 1718. The *QAR* wreckage was believed to have been found off the North Carolina coast, near Morehead City, in 1996. It has since been added to the National Register of Historic Places.

When *La Concorde de Nantes* was captured, Blackbeard upgraded her cannonry. The ship went from 14 guns to 40 guns. Yikes!

The Red-Nosed Bomber

This famous North Carolina criminal was not bringing presents to children on Christmas Eve, he was bringing pipe bombs and violent behavior. Eric Robert Rudolph grew up in Jefferson County and is most infamously known for his bombing of Centennial Olympic Park in Atlanta during the 1996 Summer Olympics, killing two people and injuring well over a hundred. He also bombed an abortion clinic, a lesbian nightclub and a family-planning clinic. Once known as the nation's most wanted domestic terrorist, Rudolph was apprehended in Murphy on May 21, 2003.

Fatal Vision

Okay, the story of Green Beret surgeon Captain Jeffrey MacDonald has been stirring up controversy ever since tragedy hit the Fort Bragg base on February 17, 1970. MacDonald's pregnant wife Colette and their two young children (five-year-old Kimberley and two-year-old Kristen) were brutally stabbed and beaten to death in their on-base apartment. MacDonald was found with a stab wound and a punctured lung. He claimed that assailants had invaded the family's home and brutally attacked them. The invaders supposedly also wrote "Pig" on the headboard of MacDonald's bed in blood. However, the army's Criminal Investigations Division (CID) did not agree with MacDonald's side of the story, thanks in part to several holes in his tale. Also, blood evidence directly refuted the captain's story, according to the Army. On May 1, 1970, MacDonald was arrested and charged with the murders of his family. He maintains his innocence to this very day.

DID YOU KNOW?

MacDonald's story was turned into a book, *Fatal Vision*, written by Joe McGinniss in 1983. The book was then made into a miniseries, starring Gary Cole as MacDonald, along with Eva

Marie Saint and Karl Malden. MacDonald actually handpicked McGinniss to write the book and then sued him for fraud. The former Green Beret claimed that McGinniss did not portray him as sympathetically as he thought he should have been.

Arsenic and Old Lace

North Carolina's own "black widow," Margie Velma Barfield was well known across the country near the end of her life. In December 1978, she was arrested and charged with first-degree murder in the death of her fiancé, Stuart Taylor. Barfield allegedly put arsenic in his beer (what a waste of good hops). Even though she wasn't tried for the crimes, she also admitted to killing her mother and three other people she was hired to care for. Her trial was something of a show, with the nation's "deadliest prosecutor" at the time—Joe Freeman Britt—leading the charge. After repeated appeals and denied motions, the convicted murderess was executed on November 2, 1984, at Central Prison in Raleigh. She was 52 years old.

DID YOU  KNOW?

Barfield was the first woman in United States history to die by lethal injection. Her last meal consisted of a Coca-Cola and Cheez Doodles.

The Rob Roys and Robin Hoods of Robeson County

The Lowry War is considered by some to be one of the most controversial happenings in North Carolina history. During the Civil War, many Cherokee and Tuscarora Indians, along with free "men of color" were conscripted to help the Confederate Home Guard build fortifications—such as Fort Fisher—near Wilmington. Several hid in the swamps and forests to avoid being captured, harassed or even murdered. The Home Guard tried, convicted and executed Allen and William Lowry (sometimes spelled Lowrie) for "allegedly" being in possession of stolen food from a neighboring homestead, as well as for harboring escaped Union war prisoners. Rumor has it that the Lowrys killed a neighbor, James Barnes, after the accusations against their family came to light. The Lowrys were mixed race (no African American blood, but obvious Native American heritage), so the rush to conviction and execution was considered yet another episode in the long line of persecution against poor, non-white residents in the South. Allen's son, Henry Berry Lowry, vowed revenge against the Home Guard and any of their supporters. He basically declared war—the Lowry War—against the richest, most affluent and most powerful people in the area. For nearly a decade, the Lowry Gang's crime spree spread terror across Robeson County and eastern North Carolina, and Lowry became the most hunted man in the state. The gang raided plantations and other wealthy areas, stealing food, money and supplies. Lowry's band of merry men (sorry for the Robin Hood reference) then shared the goods with the poor and needy people in an area called Scuffletown or the Settlement (now known as Pembroke). Lowry disappeared without a trace in 1872, and the $12,000 reward for his head was never collected.

Some view Lowry as a cultural hero who is deserving of our praise and remembrance. Others view him simply as a common criminal. Either way, the Swamp Outlaws fought for what they believed in, and the Lumbee Indians still hold him in high regard.

Since 1976, an outdoor musical drama entitled *Strike at the Wind!* has been performed in Robeson County every summer, honoring the memory of Henry Berry Lowry. There are also T-shirts, hats, signs and other paraphernalia in Robeson County that can be found, saying "Henry Berry Lowry Lives Forever."

DID YOU **KNOW?**

The tribal seat of the Lumbee Indian tribe is in Pembroke. The Lumbee are the largest tribe east of the Mississippi and the largest tribe without a reservation in the United States. They are the ninth-largest tribal nation overall, and their most important tribal honor is named after Lowry.

NOTABLE SPORTS FIGURES AND RECORD BREAKERS

Air Jordan

You can't put basketball and North Carolina in the same sentence without mentioning Michael Jordan. A native of Wilmington, Jordan helped make the sport what it is today, with his high-flying aerobatics and his confident swagger. I still remember exactly where I was when Jordan hit the winning jump shot for UNC against Georgetown in the 1982 NCAA national championship game. I also recall the battles he fought against Larry Bird and the Boston Celtics when Jordan was playing with the Chicago Bulls. We could trade important MJ moments in an entire book, but there is no doubt he dominated the basketball landscape from the mid-1980s through the 1990s—maybe even in some ways still today. Six NBA titles. Five NBA mostvaluable player awards. An NCAA national championship. Two-time college player of the year. Two Olympic gold medals. A 2009 inductee into the Naismith Hall of Fame. Yep. I think he had a minor impact or three. Jordan is now a part owner of the NBA's Charlotte Bobcats and also owns a successful car dealership in Durham. His son, Jeffrey, plays for the University of Illinois.

DID YOU KNOW?

Jordan tried his hand as an outfielder for the Birmingham Barons minor league baseball team in 1994. He played in 124 games that season and had three home runs and 114 strikeouts. He went back to the NBA the following year. I saw him play right field against the Carolina Mudcats at Five County Stadium.

North Carolina NUGGET Charlie Scott was the first African American scholarship basketball player to attend the University of North Carolina. However, there was actually one before Scott. Legendary Tar Heel coach Dean Smith gave Elm City's Willie Cooper a shot in 1964—two years before Scott enrolled at UNC. That makes Cooper the first overall African American basketball player for the Tar Heels.

Just in Case

Former North Carolina State University men's basketball coach Everett N. Case, who coached from 1946 to 1964, started the tradition of cutting down the nets after winning a championship, as well as shining a spotlight on players as they are being introduced. Nicknamed the "Old Gray Fox," Case compiled a 377–134 (.737) record over his 18 seasons—still the best in the school's history.

Many sports historians credit Case, in part, for bringing big-time basketball to North Carolina. He was inducted into the North Carolina Sports Hall of Fame in 1964 and the Naismith Memorial Basketball Hall of Fame in 1982. NC State has kept Case's memory alive by naming their main athletics office after him. The *Raleigh News & Observer* ranked Case as the most influential person in the history of North Carolina sports.

In Case You Were Wondering
Here are some other innovations on the basketball court that are attributed to Case:

☞ He began putting numbers on player jerseys.

☞ Case's teams used the full-court press for long stretches of a game.

☞ His teams would hold the ball in the backcourt to protect a lead, which eventually led to the implementation of the 10-second rule.

☞ Case would film games and review them in preparation for the next game.

☞ He played music before games.

☞ Case also invited a pep band to play at games.

Don't Give Up
When Jim Valvano was a 17-year-old high school senior, he grabbed a white index card and scribbled the following five things on it: play college basketball, become an assistant coach, become a head coach, win at Madison Square Garden in New York and cut down the nets after winning a national championship. At the age of 36, he could cross off every entry on the tattered index card, when his NC State Wolfpack defeated the University of Houston Cougars for the national title on April 4, 1983, in Albuquerque, New Mexico. A man full of humor and positive energy, Jimmy V's personality was infectious; you liked him even if you hated the Wolfpack.

The Master Motivator

In 1992, Valvano was diagnosed with metastatic adenocarcinoma, a form of cancer that begins in the cellular lining of a person's internal organs and quickly spreads to other parts of the body. Doctors told him he had less than a year to live and Valvano lived that year in typical Jimmy V style.

One of the quotes the Master Motivator is most famously known for became his life motto: "There are 86,400 seconds in a day. It's up to you to decide what to do with them." He became the poster boy for cancer awareness, hoping to help as many cancer patients as he could in the time he had left.

Here's a snippet from Jimmy V's ESPY speech, when he was given the inaugural Arthur Ashe Courage and Humanitarian Award in 1993, a short time before he lost his battle with cancer:

> *I know, I gotta go, I gotta go, and I got one last thing and I said it before and I want to say it again. Cancer can take away all my physical abilities. It cannot touch my mind, it cannot touch my heart and it cannot touch my soul. And those three things are going to carry on forever.*

Valvano's legacy and passion for cancer awareness and research lives on today through the Jimmy V Foundation for Cancer Research.

DID YOU KNOW?

Kay Yow, one of the most influential coaches in women's basketball history, also coached at North Carolina State University. In another not-so-good similarity to Jim Valvano, Yow lost a battle with cancer—breast cancer, to be specific—on January 24, 2009. With over 700 career wins and an Olympic gold medal under her belt, she's also a member of the Naismith Hall of Fame.

A King's Ransom

A member of North Carolina's first family of stock car racing, Richard Petty is probably one of the most recognized drivers in NASCAR history—maybe even in the history of all motorsports. Petty was born in Level Cross in 1937. When he turned 21 in 1958, the "King"—a name he rightfully earned—started his first NASCAR race. Petty still lives in Level Cross with his wife, Lynda. His father, Lee, won the inaugural Daytona 500 and was also a three-time NASCAR champion. Petty's son Kyle is a well-known driver as well and is a NASCAR television commentator for TNT. Adam Petty, the King's grandson, was killed in New Hampshire in 2000 while practicing in his Busch series car.

No one has made a bigger impact on the sport—on and off the track—than the King. He has been inducted into several Halls of Fame: National Motorsports Press Association Hall of Fame, International Motorsports Hall of Fame, North Carolina Auto Racing Hall of Fame, as well as the North Carolina Athletic Hall of Fame. Petty also serves as chairman of the North Carolina Motorsports Association.

The King's career spanned over 30 years, from 1958 to 1992, amassing an amazing 1185 Cup starts and 200 Cup wins. Long live the King.

A Driving Experience

Want to learn how to drive a racecar? Want to feel what it's like to climb in behind the wheel of a stock car and feel the tremble of the engine when you crank it up? Well, you don't have to be NASCAR certified to do it. Richard Petty created the Richard Petty Driving Experience (RPDE) in order to show race fans the feeling of being a NASCAR driver (or passenger). You can find the RPDE at 22 NASCAR tracks across the country.

North Carolina
NUGGET

Ever been to a stock car race and been unable to talk to the person beside you in the grandstand? What was that? Sorry, I can barely hear you over the roar of 30-plus revved-up engines flying by. Oh, okay…didn't think so. That's why it makes sense that Richard Petty is the longtime spokesman for Goody's Headache Powder.

Don't Be Intimidated

You can't mention NASCAR and not talk about number 3. Dale Earnhardt—better known as the "Intimidator"—was born in Kannapolis on April 19, 1951. Seeing his face in your rearview mirror would have been like Cole Trickle looking at Rowdy Burns in *Days of Thunder*. Earnhardt drove with an intimidating style (hence the nickname), and his black number 3 GM Goodwrench Chevrolet was always near the front of the pack. You either loved Dale or hated him—there was no in between. It's similar to J.R. Ewing from *Dallas*, or

Gabriel Gray (Sylar) from NBC's *Heroes*. Regardless of his fans or haters, Earnhardt remains one of the most popular drivers in NASCAR history.

The reign of supremacy for the seven-time Winston Cup champion came to an end at a track and during a race that had haunted him—the Daytona International Speedway (DIS). He had won every other major race at DIS except the most famous one in all of NASCAR—the Daytona 500. He finally conquered that monster in 1998. However, DIS literally claimed number 3's life in the final lap of the Daytona 500 on February 18, 2001.

NASCAR president Mike Helton broke the news to the world that evening:

> *Undoubtedly this is one of the toughest announcements I've personally had to make. After the accident in turn 4 at the end of the Daytona 500, we've lost Dale Earnhardt.*

Earnhardt's legacy lives on, as he and five other drivers (including Petty) were selected to be the inaugural inductees to the NASCAR Hall of Fame in Charlotte in May 2010. If you're ever in Kannapolis, find the Dale Trail—once there, you will definitely find that fans of number 3 continue to flock to the tiny Iredell County town to honor the life of the Intimidator.

DID YOU KNOW?

Earnhardt's first Cup race was the World 600 at the Charlotte Motor Speedway in 1978.

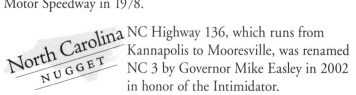

NC Highway 136, which runs from Kannapolis to Mooresville, was renamed NC 3 by Governor Mike Easley in 2002 in honor of the Intimidator.

Ride of a Lifetime

Carowinds, Charlotte's themed amusement park, will debut "The Intimidator" ride in April 2010. You guessed it—the ride's cars will be painted red and black. The ride will dominate the skyline at 232 feet in height and send you plummeting down a 211-foot first drop, then racing through more than a mile of high speed twists and turns, including seven extreme drops in excess of 75 miles per hour. Make sure you wear your Hans device.

DID YOU  **KNOW?**

Dale Earnhardt bought a minor league baseball team before his death in 2001. He bought the Piedmont Boll Weevils in 2000 and renamed them the Kannapolis Intimidators (wonder where he came up with the mascot?). In memoriam, the Intimidators retired the number 3 baseball jersey on May 15, 2002.

Awww, How Cute!
Number 3 isn't the only Earnhardt with a nickname. Dale Earnhardt Jr. is known around the racing world as "Junebug."

DID YOU  **KNOW?**

NASCAR's championship is no longer called the Winston Cup. Just ask Jimmie Johnson—he's won the last four Sprint Cup Series championships in the number 48 Lowe's Chevrolet. Johnson currently lives in Charlotte.

NOTABLE MOMENTS IN SPORTS

Cardiac Pack

The University of Houston versus NC State University. Phi Slama Jama versus the Cardiac Pack. The NCAA men's basketball championship game held on April 4, 1983, was a Cinderella story if ever there was one. The NC State Wolfpack earned the "Cardiac Pack" moniker with their nail-biting finishes, pulling off upset after upset to reach the championship game in Albuquerque, New Mexico. The Houston Cougars were number one in the country and defeated the Louisville "Doctors of Dunk" Cardinals in the Final Four. This final game was the epitome of David versus Goliath. With Houston heavily favored and facing future NBA greats Hakeem "The Dream" Olajuwon and Clyde "The Glide" Drexler, Jim Valvano and the Wolfpack never gave up, not until the very last second. NCSU's Dereck Whittenburg heaved a 30-foot prayer with time running out, and Lorenzo Charles grabbed the miss and dunked it home as the final grains of sand fell though the hourglass. The final score—NC State 54, Houston 52. That shot is one of the most replayed highlights in basketball history, as well as the shot of Jimmy V running across the court with his arms outstretched, looking for "somebody to hug." Wolfpack center Cozell McQueen was quoted after the game as saying, "We heard all about the Phi Slama Jama, but we stopped them with a Phi Pack Attack."

DID YOU KNOW?

Current NC State head coach Sidney Lowe was the point guard on the Cardiac Pack championship team.

North Carolina NUGGET The 1924 UNC men's basketball team, which completed a perfect 26-game season and won the national championship, had a nickname as well. They were called "The White Phantoms." The nickname ceased to be used in 1949, and Tar Heels was used exclusively beginning in 1950.

The First (and Only) NC Rose Bowl

In 1942, the United States was reeling from the effects of the attack on Pearl Harbor and the mounting tensions of World War II. It was decided that gathering large crowds of people in one central location on the West Coast for a college football game was not the best of ideas, so something had to be done. The 1942 Rose Bowl was scheduled to be played in Pasadena, California, between Oregon State University and Duke University. Bowl officials decided to move the game to Duke's Wallace Wade Stadium, and the Beavers went on to defeat the Blue Devils 20–16. This was the first (and only) time the Rose Bowl was held in any location other than Pasadena.

DID YOU KNOW?

The bust of legendary Duke head coach Wallace Wade at the entrance of the stadium is surrounded by rose bushes from the Tournament of Roses Committee in Pasadena, commemorating the 1942 Rose Bowl move.

Top Pic

Brian Piccolo, a running back for Wake Forest University in the early 1960s, led the nation in rushing yards and scoring during his senior season. Piccolo went on to play four seasons with the Chicago Bears—alongside NFL legend Gale Sayers—until he was diagnosed with terminal cancer. The 26-year-old Massachusetts native lost his battle against embryonic cell carcinoma on June 16, 1970. After Piccolo's death, then-director of alumni affairs Bill Joyner said, "Pic had the kind of zest for life, appreciation for tradition and reverence for the game he loved that kids used to look up to. Perhaps hero worship is childish. If it is, then I'm childish, for Pic was a hero of mine and I, along with thousands of other alumni, will miss him immeasurably."

DID YOU KNOW?

A movie was made about Piccolo's life entitled *Brian's Song*, starring James Caan as Piccolo and Billy Dee Williams as Sayers. When I was involved with the football program at Wake Forest, it was one of the first things I was shown as a freshman.

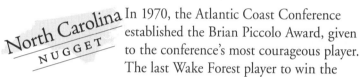

In 1970, the Atlantic Coast Conference established the Brian Piccolo Award, given to the conference's most courageous player. The last Wake Forest player to win the Piccolo was defensive end Matt Robinson in 2007. Four Demon Deacons in all have won the award since its inception.

DID YOU KNOW?

George Herman Ruth was one of baseball's most prolific sluggers. On March 7, 1914, he hit his first official major league home run in Fayetteville at the age of 19. The other players on the team heckled him because he was such a youngster and began calling him "Babe." I guess the name stuck.

Pitching Prowess
The only brothers to ever receive Major League Baseball's Cy Young Award for pitching excellence are Jim and Gaylord Perry—born in Williamston.

The "Appling" of Chicago's Eye

High Point native Lucius Benjamin "Luke" Appling Jr. was voted the greatest Chicago White Sox player of all time in a poll conducted by the Chicago Baseball Writers in 1970. Appling played his entire career for Chicago and was known in Comiskey Park by the nickname "Old Aches and Pains." He was inducted into the Baseball Hall of Fame in 1964.

POPULAR SPORTS IN THE STATE

Professionally Speaking

North Carolinians are not shy to express their preference for collegiate athletics. However, the state does boast its fair share of professional sports options. As of 2008, most professional sports were represented here, with the exception of a Major League baseball team. If you're jonesing for a pro sport, check out one of these options: NFL, NBA, minor league baseball (there are 10 minor league teams in the state, but no MLB—what's up with that?), NHL, minor league hockey, roller derby (the Carolina Rollergirls kick butt—literally), rugby, soccer and Australian rules football.

Tobacco Road

At one point, four of the biggest and most powerful university athletic programs were no more than 25 miles from each other and each was less than six miles from Interstate 40—known as "Tobacco Road." I-40 got that moniker because of North Carolina's dominance in flue-cured tobacco production. All four schools are currently members of the Atlantic Coast Conference and have been beating up on each other for as long as most North Carolinians can remember.

Those four schools are:

☛ **Duke University (Durham)**
Mascot: Blue Devils
Colors: Duke blue and white
Home Stadium (basketball): Cameron Indoor Stadium
Home Stadium (football): Wallace Wade Stadium

☛ **North Carolina State University (Raleigh)**
Mascot: Wolfpack
Colors: Red and white
Home Stadium (basketball): RBC Center
Home Stadium (football): Carter-Finley Stadium

☛ **University of North Carolina (Chapel Hill)**
Mascot: Tar Heels
Colors: Sky blue and white
Home Stadium (basketball): Dean E. Smith Center
Home Stadium (football): Kenan Stadium

☛ **Wake Forest University (Winston-Salem)**
Mascot: Demon Deacons
Colors: Old Gold and black
Home Stadium (basketball): Lawrence Joel Veterans Memorial Coliseum
Home Stadium (football): BB&T Field

Sing It!

NC State's "Red and White Song" mentions all four Tobacco Road schools.

We're the Red and White from State,
And we know we are the best.
A hand behind our back,
We can take on all the rest.
Come over the hill, Caroline.
Devils and Deacs stand in line.
The Red and White from NC State,
Go State!

Most State fans replace the "Come over the hill, Caroline" lyric with a not-so-nice one—"Go to hell, Carolina!" This change epitomizes the rivalry between UNC and NCSU.

Slam Dunk

Most people around the country look at North Carolina as a major hub for college basketball. When I moved to the West Coast in 1996, I saw more UNC and Duke jerseys in Spokane, Washington, than Washington State or even the University of Washington. That always struck me as weird. The entire state of North Carolina shuts down during March Madness. Seriously. Bars are packed with rabid fans watching their respective teams. People care more about who is going to face Duke in the first round than what's for dinner, what bills are paid and so on. I remember, in eighth grade, my teachers would use the tournament as an incentive. I can hear my English teacher now, "If the entire class makes an A on their essays, you can all watch the tournament." I never worked so hard on an essay in my life.

Krzyz-what?

Krzyzewskiville, or K-ville for short, is a phenomenon that occurs at Duke before their heated rivalry basketball game against UNC. Students camp out with tents and sleeping bags for several days before the game, in a designated area outside Cameron Indoor Stadium. Students perform in various activities (Duke Trivia, Diggin' Dirt on UNC players and Dash to the Secret Spot) in order to get points toward preferential tent order. The better your place in line, the better seat you'll get for the game. Even though K-Ville has wireless Internet, phones and laptops are prohibited for the ordering activities (students say the Internet is unreliable, anyway).

DID YOU KNOW?

The official phonetic pronunciation for Duke men's basketball coach Mike Krzyzewski's last name is *sh-SHEF-skee.*

Tee It Up!
Following closely behind college basketball as one of the most recognized sports in the state, golf is almost synonymous with

Tar Heel living. There are more than 550 courses (including both public access and private) scattered across the state, so there should be no trouble finding a driving range or a putting green. Pinehurst No. 2 is probably the most famous course in all of North Carolina, but there are many local favorites to choose from. Few other states can boast coastal, heartland and true mountain golf courses, so North Carolina is about as close as it gets to Heaven on Earth for golf enthusiasts. Several courses, including Pinehurst No. 2, are ranked on *Golf Digest's* Top 100 courses in the nation.

 Wake Forest alum Arnold Palmer captured the green jacket at the Masters a total of four times.

DID YOU KNOW?

When the 17th hole at the Black Mountain Golf Course was constructed in 1962, it was the longest golf hole in the world at the time—a par 6 adventure, spanning 747 yards.

Betcha Can't Make That Putt!

The first quintessential miniature golf course in America was designed in 1916 by James Barber in Pinehurst. Rumor has it that when Barber saw the finished course, he told the designer, "This'll do!" and the name of his course design was born—Thistle Dhu. The Thistle Dhu design was the first course to enter mass production across the U.S.

Wrestlemania

Vince McMahon, chairman and CEO of the World Wrestling Federation, was born in Pinehurst in 1945. Additionally, several other professional wrestlers were either born in North Carolina or called the Tar Heel State home:

Andre the Giant (Ellerbe)

Charles Robinson, referee
(Charlotte)

Cody Rhodes (Charlotte)

Gregory Shane Helms
(Smithfield)

Junkyard Dog (Charlotte)

Magnum T.A. (Charlotte)

Matt and Jeff Hardy
(Cameron)

R-Truth (Charlotte)

Ric Flair (Charlotte)

Shannon Moore (Cameron)

Race to the Checkered Flag

The Dukes of Hazzard TV show in the 1980s hit rather close to home in North Carolina. Moonshine runners in the Appalachian region during Prohibition had to stay two steps in front of the Highway Patrol, and getting fast cars was the first step. The cars would be souped up, the bodies would be reinforced and other drivers would get together and make joint runs, ensuring the moonshine got to its intended location without a hitch. When they weren't running moonshine, drivers would challenge each other to see who was the fastest of them all. Starting on dirt track ovals in the late 1930s, stock car racing was born, primarily in Wilkes County.

There were problems inherent in the system, however. For 20 or so years, stock car racing had no consistent rules, just good ole boys in a free-for-all to the finish line. One man came down from Washington, DC, to Florida in an effort to change that. NASCAR (National Association for Stock Car Auto Racing) was the brainchild of legendary entrepreneur Bill France Sr. in 1948. France wanted to regulate stock car racing so that the playing field would be level. NASCAR had a rule in the beginning that all cars entered into an officially sanctioned race had to be built completely with parts available to the general public in any general auto-parts store.

Rubbed the Wrong Way!

In this memorable quote from the 1990 NASCAR film *Days of Thunder*, Harry Hogge (Robert Duvall) tells Cole Trickle (Tom Cruise) that he needs to "man up":

> *Harry Hogge:* Cole, you're wandering all over the track!
> *Cole Trickle:* Yeah, well this son of a gun just slammed into me!
> *Harry Hogge:* No, no, he didn't slam you, he didn't bump you, he didn't nudge you...he "rubbed" you. And rubbin', son, is racin'.

Pole Position

The winner of the first NASCAR Strictly Stock (now Sprint Cup) race was Jim Roper ('49 Lincoln), when driver Glenn Dunnaway ('47 Ford) was disqualified for altering his car's rear springs—a favorite bootlegger trick. Strictly, "stock" means just that—cars were raced with no modifications from the factory design. The race took place at Charlotte Speedway on June 19, 1949, and the winner's purse was $2000. Roper raced in only one more event in his NASCAR career, finishing 15th. NASCAR legend Lee Petty took part in the first race as well, finishing 17th after he crashed in lap 105.

North Carolina NUGGET Even though NASCAR's headquarters are in Daytona Beach, Florida, the corporation maintains offices in four North Carolina cities: Charlotte, Concord, Mooresville and Conover. Also, the lion's share of all NASCAR teams are based near Charlotte, considered by many to be the epicenter for stock car racing for the last six decades.

Tracking NASCAR in NC

North Carolina has had its share of official NASCAR tracks, one of which is still on the circuit schedule. I actually got to see the last race at the North Carolina Speedway in 2004 while I was news/sports director for WDNC Radio in Durham. Locally known as "The Rock," the speedway had an amazing NASCAR run, and I was privileged to be able to say goodbye to a legend.

Track	First Race	Last Race
Asheville-Weaverville Speedway	1951	1969
Bowman-Gray Stadium	1958	1971
Champion Speedway	1958	1959
Charlotte Speedway	1949	1956
Cleveland County Fairgrounds	1956	1965
Concord Speedway	1956	1964
Dog Track Speedway	1962	1966
Forsyth County Fairgrounds	1955	1955
Gastonia Fairgrounds	1958	1958
Greensboro Fairgrounds	1957	1958
Harnett Speedway	1953	1953
Harris Speedway	1964	1965
Hickory Speedway	1953	1971
Jacksonville Speedway	1957	1964
Lowe's Motor Speedway	1960	–
McCormick Field	1958	1958
New Asheville Speedway	1962	1971
North Carolina Speedway	1965	2004
North Carolina State Fairgrounds	1955	1970
North Wilkesboro Speedway	1949	1996
Occoneechee Speedway	1949	1968

Raleigh Speedway	1953	1958
Salisbury Speedway	1958	1958
Southern States Fairgrounds	1954	1961
Starlite Speedway	1966	1966
Tar Heel Speedway	1963	1963
Tri-City Speedway	1953	1955
Wilson Speedway	1951	1960

The View from the Cheap Seats

With the most storied minor league baseball team in history hailing from North Carolina—the Durham Bulls—it's rather surprising that MLB has not tried to break into this market yet. However, the 10 minor league teams here keep fans entertained and give them the home runs they're looking for. Between the Greensboro Grasshoppers, the Carolina Mudcats and the Hickory Crawdads (sounds like an à la carte meal at a seafood restaurant), not to mention the six other teams across the state, baseball fans still get to see quality hits, runs and errors. (Ask Bill Buckner—there *can* be a quality error.)

The Rose Goes in the Front, Big Guy

Bull Durham, filmed in 1988, was ranked by *Sports Illustrated* as the number-one greatest sports movie of all time. As you can guess from the title, it has a little something to do with the Durham Bulls baseball team. I was in the stands during some of the scenes. I've watched the movie a million times and can't find myself. Oh well, I guess I ended up on the cutting-room floor.

Winter Sports

North Carolina's mountain ski resorts are the number-one destination east of the Rockies. If you're dying to pick up a pair of poles and slalom down an amazingly beautiful snow-covered mountainside, then head out to one of the Tar Heel State's six stellar resorts: Appalachian Ski Mountain, Cataloochee Ski Area, Ski Beech Resort, Ski Sapphire Valley, Sugar Mountain Resort or Wolf Ridge Resort. I wouldn't have a snowball's chance on skis, but the resorts also offer snowboarding, tubing and other options for non-graceful types like myself.

Just Full of Hot Air

The Carolina BalloonFest in Statesville is the world's largest hot-air balloon rally.

FIRST AND FOREMOST

There's Gold in Them Thar Hills!

When you think of gold rushes, California usually comes to mind first. However, long before people were panning the Golden State for the golden rock, gold was found in Cabarrus County in 1799—the first reported discovery of gold in the United States.

Twelve-year-old Conrad Reed found a shiny rock in the water of Little Meadow Creek while fishing one Sunday morning in 1799 and used it for a doorstop for over three years until it was sold for $3.50. The shiny doorstop was actually the first gold found in the U.S. The 17-pound gold rock was actually worth $3600. In 1799, that wasn't too shabby. Because of Conrad's discovery, the first gold mine in the country was created. The Reed Gold Mine in Cabarrus County is a National Historic Landmark and is on the National Register of Historic Places.

Golden Hickory
President Andrew Jackson created a branch of the U.S. Mint in Charlotte in 1835 to help mint the newly found gold.

We Are Siamese, If You Please...

Probably the most widely known Siamese twins are Chang and Eng Bunker. Born in Bangkok, Thailand, on May 11, 1811, the brothers, connected by a small patch of skin on their lower chest, were named Chang ("left") and Eng ("right"). At the age of 18, the brothers were purchased by an American ship's captain and began a four-decade-long stretch in the entertainment business. Both brothers married, and together they fathered 21 children. They died on January 17, 1874. The brothers and their wives are all buried in a single plot in the White Plains Baptist Church cemetery.

He's Popular!
In 1836, Edward B. Dudley became the first North Carolina governor ever elected by popular vote.

Houston, We Don't Have a Problem
The Morehead Planetarium in Chapel Hill served as a NASA training facility from 1959 to 1975.

The Doctor Is In...

Dr. Susan Dimock became the first woman member of the North Carolina Medical Society in 1872. Born in Washington, she died in a shipwreck off the coast of England in 1875.

Case Closed
The first woman licensed to practice law in North Carolina was Tabitha Holden in 1878. She was born in Guilford County in 1854.

Duke of Space

Charles Duke, the youngest of the 12 men who walked on the moon on April 1972, was born and raised in Charlotte.

Crank That Bus!
On September 5, 1917, the Pamlico County School system inaugurated the first motorized school bus service in North Carolina.

Bridge Over Troubled Water
The first drawbridge in North Carolina and what may very well have been the first in the country, was built over the Lower Cape Fear River in 1768.

Sounds Pretty Big

Albemarle Sound is the largest freshwater sound in the world.

Head, Hands, Heart and Health!

The first 4-H Club in North Carolina was started in Ahoskie by I.O. Schaub in May 1909. It was originally called the Corn Club and had only 15 members.

Ooh-rah!

Cherry Point, the largest air base in the United States Marine Corps, is located in Havelock.

Say Cheese!

The first (and only) cheese-making factory in North Carolina is the Ashe County Cheese plant in West Jefferson. It was started in 1930 by the Kraft Corporation.

Hello Dolley!

North Carolina native Dolley Madison became the first First Lady from the Tar Heel State, when her husband James was elected the fourth president of the United States in 1809.

It's Good to Be Holmes

The town of Wendell was named after the famous American writer Oliver Wendell Holmes. However, the name is not pronounced the same way. The porters on the railroad, when the train came through town in the late 1800s, would make sure to pronounce both syllables loudly and very carefully—to make sure everyone heard them. The pronunciation stuck, and the town's name is still pronounced *wen-DELL*.

Just Hanging Around

Frankie Silver was arrested and convicted of killing her husband in 1833. The Mitchell County native was the first woman in North Carolina to be sentenced to death by hanging.

Grab Your Swim Trunks!
White Lake in Elizabethtown is called the "nation's safest beach" because there are no currents, no tides and no hazardous depressions to endanger swimmers.

Just One of the Guys
Sarah Malinda Pritchard Blalock is thought to be North Carolina's first (and only) known female soldier in the Civil War. She cut her hair, put on a man's uniform and joined the Confederate Army in 1862—right alongside her husband.

They Teach This Stuff?

Did you know there's an institute that educates drivers on the art of motorsports? NASCAR Technical Institute, located in Mooresville, is the country's first technical training school to combine a complete automotive technology program and a NASCAR-specific motorsports program. It is also the exclusive educational partner of NASCAR. Now that's a first.

TOP 10 REASONS TO LIVE IN NORTH CAROLINA

1. Total Access
This is the one thing I truly love about North Carolina. Mountains, oceans, lighthouses, waterfalls, lakes, rivers, streams, woodland, big cities, small cities, farmland, concrete jungles—there is true access to everything within this state's borders. (With the exception of a Major League Baseball team—but they're working on it.) You can see the Linville Caverns, colonial shipwrecks on the coast and one of the most impressive "green" research facilities in the world (Research Triangle Park). If you want to see it, then you can probably find it here in North Carolina.

2. The Barbecue
Everything from the rooter to the tooter. Sorry, I just had to say that again. Eastern-style or western-style, your barbecue taste buds will be satisfied beyond a shadow of a doubt in the Old North State. Lexington considers itself to be the "Barbecue Capital of the World," so somebody must think it's good. Can you imagine walking into Holt Lake BBQ in Smithfield or Little Richard's BBQ in Winston-Salem and getting a plate full of barbecue with some slaw and a sweet tea? Sorry, I just drooled a little on this page. Hope you don't mind.

3. The Sporting Events
From college basketball along Tobacco Road to the square oval of Lowe's Motor Speedway in Charlotte, sports are one of the biggest draws to the state. From NASCAR to golf at Pinehurst No. 2, from the UNC-Duke basketball rivalry to some of the best minor league baseball in the county, every sports enthusiast can find something to whoop and holler about here. Bring your Terrible Towels with you when you come—the Crazy Towel Guy at Cameron Indoor Stadium will tell you to spin it loud and proud.

4. The Beauty

There is nothing like driving the Blue Ridge Parkway in fall and seeing the mountain trees and their multicolored leaves. Being able to see blooming dogwoods near Raleigh, to smell the sweet magnolia blossoms in Winston-Salem, to see the sea oats covering the dunes near Kitty Hawk or even to see the three distinct geographical zones (mountains, the Piedmont and the Coastal Plain) across the state—those are all beautiful reasons to be here.

5. The Mountain Air

The Great Smoky Mountains and the Appalachian (*ap-puh-LATCH-un*) Mountains are two very majestic reasons to love this state, with Mount Mitchell leading the mountainous charge of beauty, history and just general awesomeness. That being said, the other mountain ranges in the state have their offerings as well, such as Pilot Mountain and the various waterfalls sprinkled along the state's western side.

6. The Atlantic Coast

The Outer Banks and the rest of the North Carolina coast are truly some of the most beautiful sights I have ever seen. With the Cape Hatteras lighthouse and others still standing guard over the Graveyard of the Atlantic, people from all over the world can feel safe to come spend time along the sandy beaches and crystal blue ocean water. There's just something about packing the car on a Saturday morning—putting suntan lotion (SPF 1000+ for me) and some beach towels in the trunk— and heading out to Emerald Isle or Kure Beach for the day.

7. The Brain Power

This one made me think. Literally. Did you know that in 2009, the Raleigh-Durham area was considered to be the metropolitan area with the most collective brainpower in the nation—based on education and intellectual environment? Three major universities (Duke, UNC and NC State), combined with one of the best research areas in the world (Research Triangle Park), should have made the choice fairly easy. Sorry, San Francisco, Oakland/, San Jose…the Bay Area will just have to do better next year.

8. The People

I've heard stories from several people who moved to North Carolina that begin, "You know, the people here are so nice! Someone just opened the door for me for no reason and told me to have a good day!" In just about every city or town in North Carolina, people have had similar experiences. The niceness and the courtesy of the people here and their desire to make outsiders feel welcome (for the most part) is one of the biggest draws to this state. It's one of those gems you'll never discover until you visit the state.

9. The History

North Carolina is one of the oldest regions in the country. Home to possibly the oldest mountain range (Appalachians) and the second oldest river (New River) in the world, plus the Home of Winged Flight and the place where Civil War General William T. Sherman ended his march, this state is steeped in historical history. And who can forget Virginia Dare?

10. The Ghost Stories

Speaking of Virginia Dare, North Carolina is crawling with ghost stories. From the Outer Banks' Ghost Walk to the Footprints of Bath, these stories traverse the entire state. Some of them can get rather creepy. I guess if a state's been around as long as North Carolina has, then it is bound to collect its fair share of unhappy paranormal activity. Where's Whoopi Goldberg when you need her? (If you don't get the reference, watch the movie *Ghost* again.)

ABOUT THE ILLUSTRATORS

Craig Howrie

Craig is a self-taught artist. His line art has been used in private events for local businesses and in a local comic book art anthology. This is the second trivia book that he has illustrated for Blue Bike Books. He is also a songwriter working feverishly at a project that will hopefully see the light of day within the next decade or so...

Roger Garcia

Roger Garcia is a self-taught artist with some formal training who specializes in cartooning and illustration. He is an immigrant from El Salvador, and during the last few years, his work has been primarily cartoons and editorial illustrations in pen and ink. Recently, he has started painting once more, focusing on simplifying the human form, using a bright minimal palette and as few elements as possible. His work can be seen in newspapers, magazines and promo material and on www.rogergarcia.ca.

Peter Tyler

Peter is a recent graduate of the Vancouver Film School's Visual Art and Design and Classical animation programs. Though his ultimate passion is in filmmaking, he is also intent on developing his draftsmanship and story-telling, with the aim of using those skills in future filmic misadventures.

Patrick Hénaff

A native of France, Patrick Hénaff is mostly self-taught and is a versatile art-ist who has explored a variety of medi-ums under many different influences. He now uses primarily pen and ink to draw and then processes the images on computer. He is particularly interested in the narrative power of pictures and tries to use them as a way to tell stories, whether he is working on comic pages, posters, illustrations, cartoons or concept art.

ABOUT THE AUTHORS

John V. Wood

John V. Wood was born in Smithfield, North Carolina, and has been involved in broadcasting and journalism for over 20 years. He has written for numerous newspapers and magazines over his career, earning himself a regional Emmy Award in the process. Some of Wood's hobbies include watching movies, listening to music, playing trivia games and spending time with his wonderful family—who refuse to play Trivial Pursuit with him. Wood lives in Willow Spring with his wife Cinnamon, stepson Dillon, stepdaughter Katherine Skye and a barnyard full of animals.

Lisa Wojna

Lisa is the author of six other non-fiction books for Blue Bike Books, including *Book of Babies* and *Bathroom Book of Christmas Trivia*. She's also the author of four other non-fiction books and has co-authored more than a dozen others. She has worked in the community newspaper industry as a writer and journalist and has traveled all over Canada from the windy prairies of Manitoba to northern British Columbia and even to the wilds of Africa. Although writing and photography have been a central part of her life for as long as she can remember, it's the people behind every story that are her motivation and give her the most fulfillment.